EXPERIENCING PLEASURE
AND PROFIT IN
BIBLE STUDY

D. L. MOODY

MOODY PRESS
CHICAGO

Library of Congress Cataloging-in-Publication Data

Moody, Dwight Lyman, 1837-1899
    Experiencing pleasure and profit in Bible Study / by D.L.
    Moody
    p. cm.
    Originally published: [S.1.] : F.H. Revell, 1895.
    ISBN 0-8024-5222-1
    1. Bible—Study. I. Title

BS600.3 .M66 2001
220'.071—dc21

                                                    00-053313

1 3 5 7 9 10 8 6 4 2
Printed in the United States of America

EXPERIENCING PLEASURE AND PROFIT IN BIBLE STUDY

CONTENTS

NOTE TO OUR READERS

The ultimate impact of any book can be measured by how well the author communicates on a particular subject. The accuracy of the message and its relevance to the reader are also critical elements that distinguish a select group of books from the multitude that are available. Most important, those books that build on the foundation of the Bible, with an over-riding goal of glorifying God, are the ones that will be of greatest value to the reader. It is these writings that will stand the test of time.

This group of books, taken from the archives of Moody Press, meets those criteria. They are clear in their presentation and easy to read and apply to your life. At the same time, they do not compromise on substance, while presenting strong arguments that remain relevant to today's readers.

The authors write with elegance and conviction; their passion will inspire you. We have chosen to use the New King James Version of the Bible, which maintains the beauty and grace of the original King James Version while being highly readable in today's language.

This series of books is part of our Life Essentials™ line of products because the books fit so well with Life Essentials' objective: to help the readers stay focused on the essentials of life by keeping God at the center of all they do, grounding them in those truths that build their faith and obedience to the triune God.

We pray that these books will bless and help you in your walk of faith, just as they have done for followers of Jesus Christ in past generations.

THE PUBLISHER

PREFACE

It is always a pleasure to speak on the subject of this volume. I think I would rather preach about the Word of God than anything else except the love of God, because I believe it is the best thing in the world.

We cannot overestimate the importance of a thorough familiarity with the Bible. I try to lose no opportunity in urging people by every means in my power to the constant study of this wonderful Book. If through the pages that follow I can reach still others and rouse them to read their Bibles, not at random but with a plan and purpose, I shall be indeed thankful.

D. L. Moody.

PART ONE

WHY STUDY THE BIBLE?

CHAPTER ONE

HOW TO DEEPEN YOUR LOVE FOR THE BIBLE

A QUICKENING THAT WILL LAST must come through the Word of God. A man stood up in one of our meetings and said he hoped for enough out of the series of meetings to last him all his life. I told him he might as well try to eat enough breakfast at one time to last him a lifetime. That is a mistake that people are making; they are running to religious meetings, and they think the meetings are going to do the work. But if these don't bring you into closer contact with the Word of God, the whole impression will be gone in three months. The more you love the Scriptures, the firmer will be your faith. There is little backsliding when people love the Bible.

If you come into closer contact with the Word, you will

gain something that will last, because the Word of God is going to endure. In Psalm 119 David prayed nine times that God would quicken him—according to His Word, His law, His judgment, His precepts, and so forth.

If I could say something that would induce Christians to have a deeper love for the Word of God, I should feel this to be the most important service that could be rendered to them. Do you ask: How can I come to love the Bible? Well, if you will only arouse yourself to the study of it, and ask God's assistance, He will assuredly help you.

GOD'S WORD AND OUR WORK

The Word and work make healthy Christians. If it be all Word and no work, people will suffer from what I may call religious gout. On the other hand, if it be all work and no Word, it will not be long before they will fall into all kinds of sin and error, so that they will do more harm than good. But if we first study the Word and then go to work, we shall be healthy, useful Christians. I never saw a fruit-bearing Christian who was not a student of the Bible. If a man neglects his Bible, he may pray and ask God to use him in His work; but God cannot make use of him, for there is not much for the Holy Spirit to work upon. We must have the Word itself, which is sharper than any two-edged sword (see Hebrews 4:12).

We have a great many prayer meetings, but there

is something just as important as prayer, and that is that we read our Bibles, that we have Bible study and Bible lectures and Bible classes, so that we may get hold of the Word of God. When I pray, I talk to God, but when I read the Bible, God is talking to me; and it is really more important that God should speak to me than that I should speak to Him.

I believe we should know better how to pray if we knew our Bibles better. What is an army good for if they don't know how to use their weapons? What is a young man starting out in the Christian work good for if he does not know how to use his Bible? A man isn't worth much in battle if he has any doubt about his weapon, and I have never found a man who has doubts about the Bible who has amounted to much in Christian work. I have seen work after work wrecked because men lost confidence in the spirit of this old Book.

WE ARE NOT FOUNTAINS OURSELVES;
BUT THE WORD OF GOD IS THE TRUE
FOUNTAIN.

If young converts want to be used of God, they must feed on His Word. Their experience may be very good and profitable at the outset, and they may help others by telling it; but if they keep on doing nothing

15

else but telling their experience, it will soon become stale and unprofitable, and people will weary of hearing the same thing over and over again. But when they have told how they have been converted, the next thing is to feed on the Word. We are not fountains ourselves, but the Word of God is the true fountain.

And if we feed on the Word, it will be so easy then to speak to others; and not only that, but we shall be growing in grace all the while, and others will take notice of our walk and conversation. So few grow because so few study. I would advise all young converts to keep as much as they can in the company of more experienced Christians. I like to keep in the society of those who know more than I do; and I never lose a chance of getting all the good I can out of them. Study the Bible carefully and prayerfully; ask of others what this passage means and what that passage means, and when you have become practically acquainted with the great truths the Scriptures contain, you will have less to fear from the world, the flesh, and the devil. You will not be disappointed in your Christian life.

IF YOU GET TIRED OF THE WORD OF
GOD, AND IT BECOMES WEARISOME TO
YOU, YOU ARE OUT OF COMMUNION
WITH HIM.

People are constantly saying: We want something new: some new doctrine, some new idea. Depend upon it, my friends, if you get tired of the Word of God, and it becomes wearisome to you, you are out of communion with Him.

When I was in Baltimore, my window looked out on an Episcopal church. The stained-glass windows were dull and uninviting by day, but when the lights shone through at night, how beautiful they were! So when the Holy Spirit touches the eyes of your understanding and you see Christ shining through the pages of the Bible, it becomes a new Book to you.

A REVELATION OF GOD'S LOVE

A young lady once took up a novel to read, but found it dull and uninteresting. Some months afterward, she was introduced to the author and in the course of time became his wife. She then found that there was something in the book, and her opinion of it changed. The change was not in the book, but in herself. She had come to know and love the writer. Some Christians read the Bible as a duty, if they read it at all; but as soon as a man or woman sees Christ as the chiefest among ten thousand, the Bible becomes the revelation of the Father's love and becomes a neverending charm. A gentleman asked another, "Do you often read the Bible?" "No," was the answer, "I frankly admit I do not love God." "No more did I," the first replied, "but God loved me."

A great many people seem to think that the Bible is out-of-date, that it is an old book, and they think it has passed its day. They say it was very good for the Dark Ages, and that there is some very good history in it, but it was not intended for the present time; we are living in a very enlightened age and men can get on very well without the Old Book; we have outgrown it.

You might just as well say that the sun, which has shone so long, is now so old that it is out-of-date, and that whenever a man builds a house he need not put any windows in it, because we have a newer light and a better light; we have gaslight and electric light. These are newer; and I would advise people, if they think the Bible is too old and worn out, when they build houses, not to put windows in them, but just to light them with electric light; that is something new and that is what they are anxious for.

A PROMISE AND PROVISION FOR EVERY SITUATION

Bear in mind there is no situation in life for which you cannot find some word of consolation in Scripture. If you are in affliction, if you are in adversity and trial, there is a promise for you. In joy and sorrow, in health and in sickness, in poverty and in riches, in every condition of life, God has a promise stored up in His Word for you. In one way or another every case is met, and the truth is commended to every man's conscience. Someone has said,

- ❖ "If you are impatient, sit down quietly and commune with Job."
- ❖ "If you are strongheaded, read of Moses and Peter."
- ❖ "If you are weak-kneed, look at Elijah."
- ❖ "If there is no song in your heart, listen to David."
- ❖ "If you are a politician, read Daniel."
- ❖ "If you are getting sordid, read Isaiah."
- ❖ "If you are chilly, read of the beloved disciple."
- ❖ "If your faith is low, read Paul."
- ❖ "If you are getting lazy, read James."
- ❖ "If you are losing sight of the future, read in Revelation of the Promised Land."

It is said that Richard Baxter, author of *The Saints' Everlasting Rest*, felt the force of miracles chiefly in his youth; in maturer years he was more impressed by fulfilled prophecy; and toward the end of his life he felt the deepest satisfaction in his own ripe experience of the power of the Gospel.

A SOURCE OF GREAT PEACE

In Psalm 119:165, we find these words: "Great peace have those who love Your law, and nothing causes them to stumble." The study of God's Word will secure peace. Take those Christians who are rooted and grounded in the Word of God, and you will find they have great peace; but those who don't study their Bible, and don't know their Bible, are easily offended when some little trouble comes, or some little persecution, and their peace is all disturbed. Just a little breath of opposition and they stumble; their peace is all gone.

Sometimes I am amazed to see how little it takes to drive all peace and comfort from some people. A slandering tongue will readily blast it. But if we have the peace of God, the world cannot take that from us. It cannot give it; it cannot destroy it. We must get it from above the world. It is the peace that Christ gives. Christ said, "Blessed is he who is not offended because of Me." Now, you will notice that wherever there is a Bible-taught Christian, one who has his Bible well marked, and who daily feeds upon the Word with prayerful meditation, he will not be easily offended.

Such are the people who are growing and working all the while. But it is the people who never open their Bibles, who never study the Scriptures, who become offended, and are wondering why they are having such a hard time. They are the persons who tell you that Christianity is not what it has been recommended to them, that they have found it is not all that we claim it to be. The real trouble is, they have not done as the Lord has told them to do. They have neglected the Word of God. If they had been studying the Word of God, they would not be in that condition. They would not have wandered these years away from God, living on the husks of the world. They have neglected to care for the new life, they haven't fed it; and the poor soul, being starved, sinks into weakness and decay, and is easily stumbled or offended. If a man is born of God, he cannot thrive without God.

⌒

WE TAKE GOOD CARE OF THIS BODY
THAT WE INHABIT FOR A DAY . . . BUT
THE INNER MAN, WHICH IS TO LIVE ON
FOREVER, IS LEAN AND STARVED.

⌒

I met a man who confessed his soul had fed on nothing for forty years. "Well," said I, "that is pretty hard for the soul—giving it nothing to feed on!" That man is a type of thousands and tens of thousands today; their poor souls are starving. We take good care of this body that we inhabit for a day, and we clothe it, and deck it, and by and by it is going into the grave to decay; but the inner man, which is to live on forever, is lean and starved. "Man shall not live by bread alone, but by every word that proceeds from the mouth of God."

THE GUIDEBOOK TO THE CHRISTIAN'S JOURNEY

If a man is traveling and does not know where he is going to, or how he is going to get there, you know he has a good deal of trouble, and does not enjoy the trip as much as if he has a guidebook at hand. It is not safe traveling, and he does not know how to make through connections. Now, the Bible is a guidebook in the journey of life, and the only one that points the way to heaven. "Your word is a lamp to my feet and a light to my path."

Let us take heed then not to refuse the light and the help it gives.

CHAPTER TWO

C

THE INSPIRED
WORD OF GOD

WE DO NOT ASK MEN AND WOMEN to believe in the Bible without inquiry. It is not natural to man to accept the things of God without question. If you are to "be ready to give a defense to everyone who asks you a reason for the hope" that is within you (1 Peter 3:15), you must first be an inquirer yourself.

But do not be a dishonest doubter, with your heart and mind set against evidence. Do not be a doubter because you think it is "intellectual"; do not ventilate your doubts. "Give us your convictions," said a German writer. "We have enough doubts of our own." Be like Thomas, who did not accept Jesus' offer to feel the nail prints in His hand and side; his heart was open to conviction. "Faith," said John McNeill, "is not to be obtained at your finger-ends."

If you are filled with the Word of God, there will not be any doubts. A lady said to me once, "Don't you have any doubts?" No, I don't have time—too much work to be done. Some people live on doubt. It is their stock-in-trade. I believe the reason there are so many Christians who are without the full evidence of the relationship, in whom you see the Christian graces cropping out only every now and then, is because the Bible is not taken for doctrine, reproof, and instruction.

PROVING THE BIBLE IS TRUE

Now the request comes, "I wish you would prove to me that the Bible is true." The Book will prove itself if you will let it; there is living power in it. "We also thank God without ceasing, because when you received the Word of God which you heard from us, you welcomed it not as the word of men, but as it is in truth, the Word of God, which also effectively works in you who believe" (1 Thessalonians 2:13). It does not need defense so much as it needs studying. The Bible can defend itself. It is not a sickly child that needs nursing.

A Christian man was once talking to a skeptic who said he did not believe the Bible. The man read certain passages, but the skeptic said again, "I don't believe a word of it." The man kept on reading until finally the skeptic was convicted; and the other added: "When I have proved a good sword, I keep using it." That is what we want today. It is not our work to make men believe. That is the work of the Holy Spirit.

A BOOK OF SALVATION AND LIFE

A man once sat down to read the Bible an hour each evening with his wife. In a few evenings, he stopped in the midst of his reading and said, "Wife, if this book is true, we are wrong." He read on, and before long, stopped again and said: "Wife, if this book is true, we are lost." Riveted to the Book and deeply anxious, he still read on, and soon exclaimed: "Wife, if this book is true, we may be saved." It was not many days before they were both converted. This is the one great end of the Book, to tell man of God's great salvation. Think of a book that can lift up our drooping spirits, that can re-create us in God's image!

It is an awful responsibility to have such a book and to neglect its warnings, to reject its teachings. It is either the savor of death unto death, or of life unto life. What if God should withdraw it, and say: "I will not trouble you with it anymore"?

WHEN WE CANNOT UNDERSTAND

You ask what you are going to do when you come to a thing you cannot understand. I thank God there is a height in that Book I do not know anything about, a depth I have never been able to fathom, and it makes

25

the Book all the more fascinating. If I could take that Book up and read it as I can any other book and understand it at one reading, I should have lost faith in it years ago. It is one of the strongest proofs that that Book must have come from God, that the sharpest men who have dug for fifty years have laid down their pens and said, "There is a depth we know nothing of."

"No Scripture," said Spurgeon, "is exhausted by a single explanation. The flowers of God's garden bloom, not only double, but sevenfold. They are continually pouring forth fresh fragrance."

A man came to me with a difficult passage some time ago and said, "Moody, what do you do with that?"

"I do not do anything with it."

"How do you understand it?"

"I do not understand it."

"How do you explain it?"

"I do not explain it."

"What do you do with it?"

"I do not do anything."

"You do not believe it, do you?"

"Oh, yes, I believe it." I told him there are lots of things I do not understand, but I believe them. I do not know anything about higher mathematics, but I believe in them. I do not understand astronomy, but I believe in astronomy. Can you tell me why the same kind of food turns into flesh, fish, hair, feathers, hoofs, fingernails—according as it is eaten by one animal or another? A man told me a while ago he could not believe a thing he had never seen. I said, "Man, did you ever see your brain?"

Dr. Talmage tells the story that one day while he was bothering his theological professor with questions about the mysteries of the Bible, the latter turned on him and said: "Mr. Talmage, you will have to let God know some things you don't."

A man once said to an infidel, "The mysteries of the Bible don't bother me. I read the Bible as I eat fish. When I am eating fish and come across a bone, I don't try to swallow it, I lay it aside. And when I am reading the Bible and come across something I can't understand, I say, 'There is a bone,' and I pass it by. But I don't throw the fish away because of the bones in it; and I don't throw my Bible away because of a few passages I can't explain."

Blaise Pascal said, "Human knowledge must be understood in order to be loved; but divine knowledge must be loved to be understood." That marks the point of failure of most critics of the Bible. They do not make their brain the servant of their heart.

CRITICS AND THEIR OBJECTIONS

Did you ever notice that the things that men criticize most about the Bible are the very things to which Christ has set His seal? Men say, "You don't believe in the story of Noah and the Flood, do you?" Well, if I give it up, I must give up the Gospel; I must give up the teachings of Jesus Christ. Christ believed in the story of Noah and connected that with His return to earth. "As it was in the days of Noah, so it will be also in the days of the Son of Man."

"You don't believe in the story of Lot and Sodom, do you?" they ask. Just as much as I believe the teachings of Jesus Christ. "As it was also in the days of Lot . . . even so will it be in the day when the Son of Man is revealed" (Luke 17:26, 28, 30).

"You don't believe in the story of Lot's wife, do you?" they ask. Christ believed it: "Remember Lot's wife." They ask, "You don't believe the story of Israel looking to a brass serpent for deliverance, do you?" Christ believed it and connected it with His own cross. "As Moses lifted up the serpent in the wilderness, even so must the Son of Man be lifted up, that whoever believes in Him should not perish but have eternal life."

"You don't believe the children of Israel were fed with manna in the desert, do you?" they ask. "Our fathers ate the manna in the desert. But Jesus said, "Most assuredly, I say to you, Moses did not give you the bread from heaven, but My Father gives you the true bread from heaven" (John 6:32).

"Well, you don't believe they drank water that came out of a rock?" Christ believed it and taught it.

They ask, "You don't believe in the story of Elijah being fed by the widow, do you?" Certainly. Christ said there were many widows in the days of Elijah, but Elijah was fed by only one widow. Christ referred to it

Himself, He set His seal to it. The Son of God believed it, and shall the servant be above his master?"

ABOUT JONAH AND THE BIG FISH

Men say, "Well, you don't believe in the story of Jonah and the whale, do you?" I want to tell you I *do* believe it. A few years ago there was a man whom someone thought a little unsound, and they didn't want him to speak on the platform at our Northfield, Massachusetts summer conference. I said, "I will soon find out whether or not he is sound." I asked him, "Do you believe the whale swallowed Jonah?" "Yes," he said, "I do." I said, "All right, then I want you to come and speak." He came and gave a lecture on Jonah. In Matthew they twice asked Jesus for a sign, and He said the only sign this generation shall have shall be the sign of Jonah "in the belly of the great fish" (see Matthew 12:39–40). He connected that with His resurrection, and I honestly believe that if we overthrow the one, we must overthrow the other.

As you get along in life and have perhaps as many friends on the other side of the river as you have on this side, you will get about as much comfort out of the story of the Resurrection as any other story in the Bible. Christ had no doubt about the story. He said His resurrection would be a sign like that given unto the Ninevites. It was the resurrected man Jonah who walked through the streets of Nineveh. It must be supposed that the men of Nineveh had heard of Jonah being thrown overboard and swallowed by a great fish.

IF GOD COULD CREATE A WORLD, I THINK HE COULD CREATE A FISH LARGE ENOUGH TO SWALLOW *A MILLION* MEN.

I think it is a master stroke of Satan to make us doubt the resurrection of Jonah. But these modern philosophers have made a discovery. They say a whale's throat is no larger than a man's fist, and it is a physical impossibility for a whale to swallow a man. The book of Jonah says that God "prepared a great fish" to swallow Jonah. Couldn't God make a fish large enough to swallow Jonah? If God could create a world, I think He could create a fish large enough to swallow *a million* men. As the old woman said, "Could He not, if He chose, prepare a man who could swallow a whale?"

A couple of these modern philosophers were going to Europe some time ago, and a Scotch friend of mine on the ship knew his Bible pretty well. They got to talking about the Bible, and one of them said: "I am a scientific man, and I have made some investigation of that Book, and I have taken up some of the statements in it, and I have examined them, and I pronounce them untrue. There is a statement in the Bible that Balaam's ass spoke. I have taken pains to examine the mouth of an ass and it is so formed that it could not speak."

My friend stood it as long as he could and then said, "Eh, mon, you make the ass and I will make him speak." The idea that God could not speak through the mouth of an ass!

ABOUT CLIPPING THE BIBLE

There is another class. It is quite fashionable for people to say, "Yes, I believe the Bible, but not the supernatural. I believe everything that corresponds with this reason of mine." They go on reading the Bible with a penknife, cutting out this and that. My answer is, "Now, if I have a right to cut out a certain portion of the Bible, I don't know why one of my friends has not a right to cut out another, and another friend to cut out another part, and so on. You would have a queer kind of Bible if everybody cut out what he wanted to."

In fact, every adulterer would cut out everything about adultery; every liar would cut out everything about lying; every drunkard would be cutting out what he didn't like.

I HAVE YET TO FIND A MAN WHO BEGINS TO PICK AT THE BIBLE THAT DOES NOT PICK IT ALL TO PIECES IN A LITTLE WHILE.

Once, a gentleman took his Bible around to his minister and said, "That is your Bible." "Why do you call it *my* Bible?" said the minister. "Well," replied the gentleman, "I have been sitting under your preaching for five years, and when you said a thing in the Bible was not authentic, I cut it out." He had about a third of the Bible cut out; all of Job, all of Ecclesiastes and Revelation, and a good deal besides. The minister wanted him to leave the Bible with him; he didn't want the rest of his congregation to see it. But the man said, "Oh, no! I have the covers left, and I will hold onto them." And off he went holding on to the covers. If you believed what some men preach, you would have nothing but the covers left in a few months. I have often said that if I am going to throw away the Bible, I will throw it all into the fire at once. There is no need of waiting five years to do what you can do as well at once. I have yet to find a man who begins to pick at the Bible that does not pick it all to pieces in a little while.

A minister whom I met a while ago said to me, "Moody, I have given up preaching except out of the four Gospels. I have given up all the epistles, and all the Old Testament; and I do not know why I cannot go to the fountainhead and preach as Paul did. I believe the Gospels are all there is that is authentic." It was not long before he gave up the four Gospels, and finally gave up the ministry. He gave up the Bible, and God gave him up.

A prophet who had been sent to a city to warn the wicked was commanded not to eat meat within its walls. He was afterward deceived into doing so by an old prophet, who told him that an angel had come to him and said he might return and eat with him. That prophet was destroyed by a lion for his disobedience (see 1 Kings 13:7–24). If an angel should come and tell a different story from that in the Book, don't believe it. I am tired of people following men. It is written, "though an angel from heaven preach any other gospel, let him be accursed." Do you think with more light before us than the prophet had that we can disobey God's Word with impunity?

ABOUT THE SUPERNATURAL IN THE BIBLE

It is a most absurd statement for a man to say he will have nothing to do with the supernatural, will not believe the supernatural. If you are going to throw off the supernatural, you might as well burn your Bibles at once. You take the supernatural out of that Book and you have taken Jesus Christ out of it; you have taken out the best part of the Book. There is no part of the Bible that does not teach supernatural things. In Genesis it says that Abraham fell on his face and God talked with him. That is supernatural. If that did not take place, the man who wrote Genesis wrote a lie, and out goes Genesis. In Exodus you find the ten plagues which came upon Egypt. If that is not true, the writer of Exodus was a liar. Then in Leviticus it is said that fire consumed the two sons of Aaron. That was a supernatural event, and if that was not true, we must throw out the whole Book.

In Numbers is the story of the brazen serpent. And so with every book in the Old Testament; there is not one in which you do not find something supernatural. There are more supernatural things about Jesus Christ than in any other portion of the Bible, and the last thing a man is willing to give up is the four Gospels. Five hundred years before His birth, the angel Gabriel came down and told Daniel that He should be born (see Daniel 9:21, 25). Centuries later, Gabriel came down to Nazareth and told the virgin that she should be the mother of the Savior. "Behold, you will conceive in your womb and bring forth a Son, and shall call His name Jesus" (Luke 1:31). We find, too, that the angel went into the temple and told Zacharias that he was to be the father of John the Baptist, the forerunner of the Messiah; Zacharias was struck dumb for nine months because of his unbelief.

Then when Christ was born, we find angels appearing to the shepherds at Bethlehem, telling them of the birth of the Savior. "For there is born to you this day in the city of David a Savior, who is Christ the Lord." The wise men seeing the star in the east and following it was surely supernatural. So was the warning that God sent to Joseph in a dream, telling him to flee to Egypt. So was the fact of our Lord's going into the temple at the age of twelve, discussing with the teachers, and being a match for them all. So were the circumstances attending His baptism, when God spoke from heaven, saying: "This is My beloved Son."

> WHEN HE DIED, THE SUN REFUSED TO
> LOOK UPON THE SCENE; THIS OLD
> WORLD RECOGNIZED HIM AND REELED
> AND ROCKED LIKE A DRUNKEN MAN.

For three and a half years, Jesus trod the streets and highways of Palestine. Think of the many wonderful miracles that He wrought during those years. One day He spoke to the leper and he was made whole; one day He spoke to the sea and it obeyed Him. When He died, the sun refused to look upon the scene; this old world recognized Him and reeled and rocked like a drunken man. And when He burst asunder the bands of death and came out of Joseph's sepulchre, that was supernatural. Christmas Evans, the great Welsh preacher, said: "Many reformations die with the reformer, but this reformer ever lives to carry on His reformation." Thank God we do not worship a dead Jew. If we worshipped a dead Jew, we would not have been quickened and have received life in our souls.

I thank God our Christ is a supernatural Christ, and this Book a supernatural Book, and I thank God I live in a country where it is so free that all men can read it.

Some people think we are deluded, that this is imagination. Well, it is a glorious imagination, is it not? It has lasted now going on forty years with me, and I think it is going to last while I live, and when I go into another world. Someone, when reading about

Paul, said he was mad. Well, it was replied, if he was, he had a good keeper on the way, and a good asylum at the end of the route. I wish we had a lot of madmen in America just like Paul.

ABOUT INSPIRATION

When Paul wrote to Timothy that *all* Scripture "is given by inspiration of God, and is profitable" (2 Timothy 3:16), he meant what he said. "Well," some say, "do you believe all Scripture is given by inspiration?" Yes, every word of it; but I don't believe all the action and incidents it tells of were inspired. For instance, when the devil told a lie he was not inspired to tell a lie, and when a wicked man like Ahab said anything, he was not inspired; but someone was inspired to write it, and so all was given by inspiration and is profitable.

LET THE WORD OF GOD INTO YOUR
SOUL, AND IT WILL INSPIRE YOU.

Peter tells us, regarding salvation through the sufferings of Christ: "Of this salvation the prophets have inquired and searched carefully, who prophesied of the grace that would come to you, searching what, or what manner of time, the Spirit of Christ who was in them was indicating when He testified beforehand the sufferings of Christ and the glories that would follow"

(1 Peter 1:10–11). So the prophets themselves had to inquire and search diligently regarding the words they uttered under the inspiration of the Spirit.

A man said to a young convert: "How can you prove that the Bible is inspired?" He replied, "Because it inspires me." I think that is pretty good proof. Let the Word of God into your soul, and it will inspire you. It cannot help it.

CHAPTER THREE

THE WHOLE BIBLE: THE OLD AND NEW TESTAMENTS

WHEN SPEAKING OF THE LAW, Christ said: "One jot or one tittle will by no means pass from the law till all is fulfilled." In another place He said, "Heaven and earth will pass away, but My words will by no means pass away."

Now, let us keep in mind that the only Scripture the apostles and Christ had was the Old Testament. The New Testament was not written. I will put that as the old and new covenant. "One jot or one tittle will by no means pass from the law till all is fulfilled"—the old covenant. Then Christ came, adding these words: "Heaven and earth will pass away, but My words will by no means pass away"—the new covenant. Notice how that *has* been fulfilled.

I can see one of your modern freethinkers standing near Him, and he hears Christ say: "Heaven and earth will pass away, but My words will by no means pass away." I see the scornful look on his face as he says: "Hear that Jewish peasant talk! Did you ever hear such conceit, such madness? He says heaven and earth shall pass away, but His words shall not pass away." My friend, I want to ask you this question: Have they passed away? Do you know that the sun has shone on more Bibles today than ever before in the history of the world? There have been more Bibles printed in the last ten years than in the first eighteen hundred years.

THE EVER-PRESENT WORD OF GOD

They tried in the Dark Ages to chain it and keep it from the nations, but God has preserved it, and the British and American Bible Societies print thousands of Bibles every day. One publisher in New York has sold one hundred thousand Bibles during the last year.

Suppose someone had said that when we had a revised version of the New Testament, it was going to have such a large circulation—people reading it wherever the English language is spoken—the statement would hardly have been believed. The new version came out in New York on a Friday, on the same day that it was published in London. Chicago did not want to be behind New York. At that time the quickest train between the two cities could not accomplish the journey in less than about twenty-six hours. It would be late on Saturday afternoon before the copies could reach Chicago, and the stores would be closed. So one of the Chicago daily papers set ninety operators at work and had the whole of the new version, from Matthew to Revelation, telegraphed to Chicago on Friday; it was put at once into print and sold on the streets of Chicago the next day. If someone had said years ago, before telegrams were introduced, that this would be done, it would have been thought an impossibility. Yet it has been done.

Notwithstanding all that skeptics and infidels say against the Old Book, it goes on its way. These objectors remind one of a dog barking at the moon; the moon goes on shining just the same. Atheists keep on writing against the Bible; but they do not make much progress, do they? It is being spread abroad—silently, and without any blasts of trumpets. The lighthouse does not blow a trumpet; it goes on shedding its light all around. So the Bible is lighting up the nations of the earth. It is said that a lecturer on secularism was once asked, "Why can't you let the Bible alone, if you don't believe it?" The honest reply was at once made, "Because the Bible won't let me alone."

THE WORD IS GOING TO LIVE, AND THERE IS NO POWER IN PERDITION OR EARTH THAT CAN BLOT IT OUT.

The Bible was the first book ever printed; in any day New Testaments are printed in 353 different languages, and are going to the very corners of the earth. Wherever the Bible has not been translated, the people have no literature. It will not be long before the words of Jesus Christ will penetrate the darkest parts of the earth, and the darkest islands of the sea.

When Christ said, "The Scripture cannot be broken," He meant every word He said. Devil and man and hell have been in league for centuries to try to break the Word of God, but they cannot do it. If you get it for your footing, you have good footing for time and eternity. "Heaven and earth will pass away, but My words will by no means pass away." My friends, the Word is going to live, and there is no power in perdition or earth that can blot it out.

BELIEVING THE WHOLE BIBLE

What we want today are men and women who believe in the Bible from the crown of their heads to the soles of their feet, who believe the whole of it, the things they understand and the things they do not understand. Talk about the things you understand, and leave the things you do not. I believe that is one reason why the English and the Scotch Christians have gotten ahead of us, because they study the whole Bible. I venture to say that there are hundreds of Bible readings in London every night. You know there are a good many Christians who are good in some spots and mighty poor in other spots, because they do not take the whole sweep of the Bible. When I went to Scotland I had to be very careful how I quoted the Bible. Some friend would tell me after the meeting I was quoting it wrong.

I want to say how absurd it is for anyone to say he believes the New Testament and not the Old. Of the thirty-nine books of the Old Testament, it is recorded that our Lord made quotations from no less than twenty-two. Very possibly He may have quoted from all of them; for we have only fragments recorded of what He said and did. You know the apostle John tells us that the world could scarcely contain the books that could be written, if all the sayings and doings of our Lord were recorded (see John 21:25). About eight hundred and fifty passages in the Old Testament are quoted or alluded to in the New, only a few occurring more than once.

In the gospel by Matthew there are over a hundred quotations from twenty of the books in the Old Testament. In the gospel of Mark there are fifteen quotations taken from thirteen of the books. In the gospel of Luke there are thirty-four quotations from thirteen books. In the gospel of John there are eleven quotations from six books. In the four Gospels alone there are more than one hundred and sixty quotations from the Old Testament. You sometimes hear men saying they do not believe all the Bible, but they believe the teaching of Jesus Christ in the four Gospels. Well, if I

43

believe that, I have to accept these hundred and sixty quotations from the Old Testament.

In Paul's letters to the Corinthians there are fifty-three quotations from the Old Testament; sometimes he takes whole paragraphs from it. In Hebrews there are eighty-five quotations in that one book of thirteen chapters. In Galatians, sixteen quotations. In the book of Revelation alone, there are two hundred and forty-five quotations and allusions.

THE OLD TESTAMENT UNDER ATTACK

A great many want to throw out the Old Testament. It is a good historic reading, they say, but they don't believe it is a part of the Word of God, and don't regard it as essential in the scheme of salvation. The last letter Paul wrote contained the following words: "And that from childhood you have known the Holy Scriptures, which are able to make you wise for salvation through faith which is in Christ Jesus." All the Scriptures which the apostles possessed were of the Old Testament.

CHRIST GAVE HIMSELF UP AS A SACRIFICE THAT THE SCRIPTURES MIGHT BE FULFILLED.

When skeptics attack its truths, these find it convenient to say, "Well, we don't endorse all that is in the Old Testament," and thus they avoid an argument in defense of the Scriptures. It is very important that every Christian should not only know what the Old Testament teaches, but he should accept its truths, because it is upon this Testament that truth is based. Peter said the Scriptures are not given for any private interpretation, and in speaking of the Scriptures, referred to the Old Testament and not to the New.

If the Old Testament Scriptures are not true, do you think Christ would have so often referred to them, and said the Scriptures must be fulfilled? When told by the tempter that He might call down the angels from heaven to interpose in His behalf, He said: "It is written." Christ gave Himself up as a sacrifice that the Scriptures might be fulfilled. Was it not said that He was numbered with the transgressors?

When He talked with two of His disciples on the way while journeying to Emmaus after His resurrection, did He not say: "Ought not these things to be? Am I not to suffer?" And beginning at Moses He explained unto them in all the Scriptures concerning Himself, for the one theme of the Old Testament is the Messiah. In Psalm 40:7, it says: "In the volume of the book it is written of me" (KJV). "What *Book?*" asks Luther, "and what *Person?* There is only one book—the Bible; and only one person—Jesus Christ."

IF JESUS CHRIST COULD USE THE OLD TESTAMENT, LET US USE IT.

Christ referred to the Scriptures and their fulfillment in Him, not only after He arose from the dead, but in the book of Revelation He used them in heaven. He spoke to John of them on the Isle of Patmos, and used the very things in them that men are trying to cast out. He never found fault with or rejected them.

If Jesus Christ could use the Old Testament, let us use it. May God deliver us from the one-sided Christian who reads only the New Testament and talks against the Old!

CHAPTER FOUR

FULFILLED PROPHECIES

I KNOW NOTHING THAT WILL upset an honest skeptic quicker than fulfilled prophecy. There are very few Christians who think of studying this subject. They say that prophecies are so mysterious, and there is question about their being fulfilled.

Now the Bible does not say that prophecy is a dark subject, to be avoided; but rather that "we have the prophetic word confirmed, which you do well to heed as a light that shines in a dark place, until the day dawns and the morning star rises in your hearts" (2 Peter 1:19). Prophecy is history unfulfilled, and history is prophecy fulfilled.

When I was a boy, I was taught that all beyond the Mississippi River was the great American desert. But when the first pickax struck into the Comstock Lode, and they took out more than one hundred million dollars' worth of silver, the nation realized that there was no desert; and that part of the country—Nevada, Colorado, Utah, and other western states—became the most valuable we possess. Think of the busy cities and flourishing states that have sprung up among the mountains! So with many portions of the Bible: People never think of reading them. They are living on a few verses and chapters. The greater part of the Bible was written by prophets, yet you seldom hear a sermon preached on prophecy.

Between five and six hundred Old Testament prophecies have been remarkably and literally fulfilled, and two hundred in regard to Jesus Christ alone. Not a thing happened to Jesus Christ that was not prophesied from seventeen hundred to four hundred years before He was born.

Take the four great cities that existed in the days when the Old Testament was written, and you will find that prophecies regarding them have been fulfilled to the letter. Let me call your attention to a few passages.

PROPHECIES ABOUT THE BABYLONIAN EMPIRE

First, regarding Babylon:

Babylon, the glory of kingdoms, the beauty of the Chaldeans' pride, will be as when God overthrew Sodom and Gomorrah. It will never be inhabited, nor will it be settled from generation to generation; nor will the Arabian pitch tents there, nor will the shepherds make their sheepfolds there. But wild beasts of the desert will lie there, and their houses will be full of owls; ostriches will dwell there, and wild goats will caper there. The hyenas will howl in their citadels, and jackals in their pleasant places. Her time is near to come, and her days will not be prolonged. (Isaiah 13:19–22)

And again, here is a similar prophecy, this time from Jeremiah:

The word that the Lord spoke against Babylon and against the land of the Chaldeans by Jeremiah the prophet. "Declare among the nations, proclaim, and set up a standard; proclaim— do not conceal it—say, 'Babylon is taken, Bel is shamed, Merodach is broken in pieces; her idols are humiliated, her images are broken in pieces.' For out of the north a nation comes up against her; which shall make her land desolate, and no one shall dwell therein; they shall move, they shall depart, both man and beast. . . . Because of the wrath of the Lord, she shall not be inhabited, but she shall be wholly desolate. Everyone who goes by Babylon shall be horrified, and hiss at all her plagues. . . . How the hammer of the whole earth has been cut apart and broken! How Babylon has become a desolation among the nations! I have laid a snare for you; you have indeed been trapped, O Babylon, and you were not aware; you have been found and also caught, because you have contended against the Lord." (Jeremiah 50:1–3, 13, 23–24)

WHEN BABYLON WAS IN ITS GLORY . . . PROPHETS PREDICTED THAT IT WOULD BE DESTROYED. HOW LITERALLY WAS IT FULFILLED!

A hundred years before Nebuchadnezzar ascended the throne, it was foretold how Babylon should be destroyed, and it came to pass. Scholars tell us that the city stood in the midst of a large and fruitful plain. It was enclosed by a wall four hundred and eighty furlongs square. Each side of the square had twenty gates of solid brass, and at every corner was a strong tower, ten feet higher than the wall. The wall was eighty-seven feet broad, and three hundred and fifty feet high. These figures give an idea of the importance of Babylon. Yet nothing but ruins now remain to tell of its former grandeur. When Babylon was in its glory, the queen of the earth, prophets predicted that it would be destroyed. How literally was it fulfilled!

A friend going through the valley of the Euphrates tried to get his guide to pitch his tent near the ruins and failed. No Arabian pitches his tent there; no shepherd will dwell near the ruins.

PROPHECIES ABOUT THE CITIES OF NINEVEH, TYRE, AND JERUSALEM

Now take Nineveh. "I will cast abominable filth upon

you, make you vile, and make you a spectacle. It shall come to pass that all who look upon you will flee from you, and say, 'Nineveh is laid waste! Who will bemoan her?' Where shall I seek comforters for you?" (Nahum 3:6–7).

"I will cast upon her abominable filth," God said. Now, how are you going to cover the city up? And yet for 2,500 years Nineveh was buried and an abominable filth lay upon her. But they have dug up the ruins, and brought them to Paris and London, and you go into the British museum, and there is not a day except the Sabbath but what you can see men from all parts of the world gazing upon the ruins. It is just as the prophets prophesied. For 2,500 years Nineveh was buried, but it is no longer buried.

Then look at Tyre:

"Therefore thus says the Lord God: 'Behold, I am against you, O Tyre, and will cause many nations to come up against you, as the sea causes its waves to come up. And they shall destroy the walls of Tyre and break down her towers; I will also scrape her dust from her, and make her like the top of a rock. It shall be a place for spreading of nets in the midst of the sea, for I have spoken,' says the Lord God; 'it shall become plunder for the nations.'" (Ezekiel 26:3–5)

WHEN THEY PROPHESIED AGAINST THESE GREAT CITIES, THEY WERE LIKE LONDON, PARIS, AND NEW YORK IN THEIR GLORY, BUT THEIR GLORY HAS GONE.

Coffin, a correspondent of the *Boston Journal* during the war, went around the world after the war was over in 1868. One night he came to the site of old Tyre, and he said the sun was just going down, and he got his guide to pitch his tent right over by the ruins, where the rocks were scraped bare, and he took out his Bible and read where it says, "It shall be a place for the spreading of nets."

He said the fishermen had finished fishing and were just spreading their nets on the rocks of Tyre, precisely as it was prophesied hundreds and hundreds of years before. Now, mark you! When they prophesied against these great cities, they were like London, Paris, and New York in their glory, but their glory has gone.

Now take the prophecy in regard to Jerusalem.

> *Now as He drew near, He saw the city and wept over it, saying, "If you had known, even you, especially in your day, the things that make for your peace! But now they are hidden from your eyes. For the days will come upon you when your enemies will build an embankment around you, surround you and close you in on every side." (Luke 19:41–43)*

Didn't Titus do that? Didn't the Roman emperor do that very thing?

Jesus then completed the prophecy: "And level you, and your children within you, to the ground . . . because you did not know the time of your visitation" (verse 44).

I read of two rabbis going up to Jerusalem, and

they saw a fox playing upon the wall; one began to weep when he thus looked at the desolation of Zion. The other smiled and rebuked him, saying that the spectacle was a proof that the Word of God was true, and that this was one of the prophecies which should be fulfilled—"Because of the mountain of Zion, which is desolate, the foxes walk upon it" (Lamentations 5:18 KJV). It was also said that Jerusalem should be as a plowed field. This prophecy has also been fulfilled. The city became so restricted that outside of the walls, where part of the old city stood, the plow has been used.

PROPHECIES ABOUT EGYPT

Now take the prophecies regarding Egypt: "It shall be the lowliest of kingdoms; it shall never again exalt itself above the nations, for I will diminish them so that they will not rule over the nations anymore" (Ezekiel 29:15). Now, mark you! Egypt was in its glory when this was prophesied. It was a great and mighty empire, but for centuries it has been the lesser of nations. They have not a native prince or king to reign over them.

PROPHECIES ABOUT THE JEWISH PEOPLE

Then, again, the prophecy of Balaam with regard to the Jews has been already greatly fulfilled. "There! A people dwelling alone, not reckoning itself among the nations. Who can count the dust of Jacob, or number one-fourth of Israel?" (Numbers 23:9–10). The Jews were not to be reckoned among the nations. There is something in this people's looks and habits that God continues to perpetuate, just, as I believe, to make them witnesses in every land of the truth of the Bible.

THE PROPHECY IS FULFILLED—GOD HAS MADE THE NATION NUMEROUS AND UNITED.

The race has remained all these centuries separate and distinct from other nations. In America there are all kinds of nationalities. Take an Irishman, and in a generation he will have forgotten his nationality. So, too, with the Germans, Italians, and French; but the Jew is as much a Jew as he was when he came long years ago. See how the race has been persecuted, yet the Jews . . . cannot be kept down. Egypt, Edom, Assyria, Babylon, Persia, Rome, and all the leading nations of the earth have sought to crush the Jews. Frederick the Great said, "Touch them not, for no one has done so and prospered." The people are the same now as they were in the days of Pharaoh, when he tried to destroy all the male children. The prophecy is fulfilled—God has made the nation numerous and united.

The time is coming when God will reinstate the

Jew. "For the children of Israel shall abide many days without king or prince, without sacrifice or sacred pillar, without ephod or teraphim" (Hosea 3:4). Are they not without a king and without a sacrifice? Are they not scattered among the nations of the earth, yet a separate and distinct people? Their King they crucified. They will not have another until they restore Him. He was Jesus Christ, as inscribed upon His cross, "The King of the Jews."

OTHER PROPHECIES

We see how it was prophesied that Eli should suffer. He was God's own high priest, and the only thing against him was that he did not obey God's Word faithfully and diligently. He was like a good many people. He was one of these good-natured old men who don't want to make people uncomfortable by saying unpleasant things, so he let his two boys go on in neglect, and did not restrain them. He was just like some ministers. Oh, let every minister tell the truth, though he preach himself out of his pulpit. Everything went all right for twenty years, but then came fulfillment of the prophecy. God's ark was taken, the army of Israel was routed by the Philistines, Hophni and Phinehas, old Eli's two sons, were killed, and when the old man heard of it, he fell back in his chair, broke his neck, and died (see 1 Samuel 4:10–18).

So with King Ahab, taking the sinful advice of Jezebel. Naboth would not sell him that piece of land,

55

so they got him out of the way. Three years afterward the dogs licked Ahab's blood from his chariot in the very spot where Naboth's had been murderously shed, according to Elijah's prophecy (see 1 Kings 21:19; 22:38).

CHAPTER FIVE

_C_

POWER AND PROFIT
IN PREACHING THE BIBLE

_H_ERE IS A WORD OF COUNSEL for young men who have their eye on the ministry. If you take my advice, you will seek not to be a text preacher but an expository preacher. I believe that what this country wants is the Word of God. There is no book that will draw the people like the Bible. One of the professors of a nearby university gave some lectures on the Book of Job, and there was no building large enough to hold the people. If the Bible only has a chance to speak for itself, it will interest the people.

I am tired and sick of moral essays. It would take about a ton of them to convert a child five years old. A man was talking of a certain church once and said he liked it because the preacher never touched on politics and religion—just read nice little essays. Give the people the Word of God. Some men only use the Bible as a textbook. They get a text and away they go. They go up in a balloon and talk about astronomy, and then go down and give you a little geology, and next Sunday they go on the same way, and then they wonder why it is people do not read their Bibles.

I used to think Charles Spurgeon was about as good a preacher as I ever knew, but I would rather hear him expound the Scripture than listen to his sermons. Why is it that Dr. John Hall holds his audience so long? He opens his Bible and expounds.

How was it that Andrew Bonar held his audience in Glasgow? He had a weak voice; people could hardly hear him, yet thirteen hundred people would file into his church twice every Sabbath, and many of them took notes, and they would go home and send his sermons all over the world. It was Dr. Bonar's custom to lead his congregation through the study of the Bible, book by book. There was not a part of the Bible in which he could not find Christ. I preached five months in Glasgow, and there was not a ward or district in the city in which I did not find the influence of that man.

PETER AND PAUL TOGETHER

I was in London in '84 and a lawyer had come down from Edinburgh. He said he went through to

Glasgow a few weeks before to spend Sunday, and he was fortunate enough to hear Andrew Bonar. He said he happened to be there the Sunday Dr. Bonar got to that part of the epistle of Galatians where it says that Paul went up to Jerusalem to see Peter. "Then after three years I went up to Jerusalem to see Peter, and remained with him fifteen days." Dr. Bonar let his imagination roam. He said one day he could imagine they had been very busy and they were tired, and all at once Peter turned to Paul and said, "Paul, wouldn't you like to take a little walk?" And Paul said he would.

So they went down through the streets of Jerusalem arm-in-arm, over the Brook Kidron, and all at once Peter stopped and said, "Look, Paul, this is the very spot where He wrestled, and where He suffered and sweat great drops of blood. There is the very spot where John and James fell asleep, right there. And right here is the very spot where I fell asleep. I don't think I should have denied Him if I hadn't gone to sleep, but I was overcome. I remember the last thing I heard Him say before I fell asleep was, 'Father, let this cup pass from me if it is Thy will.' And when I awoke an angel stood right where you are standing, talking to Him, and I saw great drops of blood come from His pores and trickle down His cheeks.

"It wasn't long before Judas came to betray Him. And I heard Him say to Judas so kindly, 'Are you betraying the Son of Man with a kiss?' And then they bound Him and led Him away. That night when He was on trial I denied Him."

"SEE THAT HOLE RIGHT THERE? THAT IS WHERE HIS CROSS STOOD."

Bonar pictured the scene. And the next day Peter turned again to Paul and said, "Wouldn't you like to take another walk today?" And Paul said he would. That day they went to Calvary, and when they got on the hill, Peter said, "Here, Paul, this is the very spot where He died for you and me. See that hole right there? That is where His cross stood. The believing thief hung there, and the unbelieving thief there on the other side. Mary Magdalene and Mary His mother stood there, and I stood away on the outskirts of the crowd. The night before when I denied Him, He looked at me so lovingly that it broke my heart, and I couldn't bear to get near enough to see Him.

"That was the darkest hour of my life. I was in hopes that God would intercede and take Him from the cross. I kept listening and I thought I would hear His voice."

Bonar pictured the whole scene, how they put the crown of thorns on His brow, and drove the spear into His side, and all that took place.

And the next day Peter turned to Paul again and asked him if he wouldn't like to take another walk.

And Paul said he would. Again they passed down the streets of Jerusalem, over the Brook Kidron, over Mount Olivet, up to Bethphage, and over on to the slope near Bethany. All at once Peter stopped and said, "Here, Paul, this is the last place where I ever saw Him. I never heard Him speak so sweetly as He did that day. It was right here He delivered His last message to us, and all at once I noticed that His feet didn't touch the ground. He arose and went up. All at once there came a cloud and received Him out of sight.

"I stood right here gazing up into the heavens, in hopes I might see Him again and hear Him speak. And two men dressed in white dropped down by our sides and stood there and said, 'Men of Galilee, why do you stand gazing up into heaven? This same Jesus, who was taken up from you into heaven, will so come in like manner as you saw Him go into heaven.'"

I MYSELF SPENT EIGHT DAYS IN JERUSALEM, AND EVERY MORNING I WANTED TO STEAL DOWN INTO THE GARDEN WHERE MY LORD SWEAT GREAT DROPS OF BLOOD.

My friends, do you believe that picture is overdrawn? Do you believe Peter had Paul as his guest and didn't take him to Gethsemane, didn't take him to Calvary and to Mount Olivet? I myself spent eight days in Jerusalem, and every morning I wanted to steal down into the garden where my Lord sweat great drops of blood. Every day I climbed Mount Olivet and looked up into the blue sky where He went to His Father. I have no doubt Peter took Paul out on those three walks. If there had been a man who could have taken me to the very spot where my Master sweat those great drops of blood, do you think I wouldn't have asked him to take me there? If he could have told me where I could find the spot where my Master's feet last touched this sin-cursed earth and was taken up, do you think I wouldn't have had him show it to me?

ORATORICAL PREACHING

I know there is a class of people who say that kind of preaching won't do in this country. "People want something oratorical." Well, there is no doubt but that there are some who want to hear oratorical sermons, but usually they forget them inside of twenty-four hours.

It is a good thing for a minister to have the reputation of feeding his people. A man once made an artificial bee, which was so like a real bee that he challenged another man to tell the difference. It made just such a buzzing as the live bee and looked the same. The other said, "You put the artificial bee and a real bee down there, and I will tell you the difference pretty quickly." He then put a drop of honey on the ground, and the live bee went for the honey. It is just so with us. There are a lot of people who profess to be Christians, but they are artificial, and they don't know when you give them honey. The real bees go for honey every time. People can get along without your theories and opinions. "Thus says the Lord"—that is what we want.

PART TWO

METHODS OF BIBLE STUDY

CHAPTER SIX

SEARCHING
THE SCRIPTURES

MERELY READING THE BIBLE is not what God wants.
Again and again I am exhorted to "search":

> *These were more fair-minded than those in Thessalonica, in that they received the word with all readiness, and searched the Scriptures daily to find out whether these things were so.* (Acts 17:11)

> *So they read distinctly from the book, in the Law of God; and they gave the sense, and helped them to understand the reading.* (Nehemiah 8:8)

SEEKING SOMETHING OF VALUE

We must study the Bible thoroughly, and hunt it through,

as it were, for some great truth. If a friend were to see me searching about a building, and were to come up and say, "Moody, what are you looking for? Have you lost something?" and I answered, "No, I haven't lost anything; I'm not looking for anything particular," I fancy he would just let me go on by myself, and think me very foolish. But if I were to say, "Yes, I have lost a dollar," why, then I might expect him to help me to find it. Read the Bible, my friends, as if you were seeking something of value. It is a good deal better to take a single chapter, and spend a month on it, than to read the Bible at random for a month.

At one time I used to read so many chapters a day, and if I did not get through my usual quantity I thought I was getting cold and backsliding. But, mind you, if a man had asked me two hours afterward what I had read, I could not tell him; I had forgotten it nearly all. When I was a boy I used, among other things, to hoe corn on a farm; and I used to hoe it so badly, in order to get over so much ground, that at night I had to put down a stick on the ground, so as to know next morning where I had left off. That was somewhat in the same fashion as running through so many chapters every day. A man will say, "Wife, did I read that chapter?" "Well," says she, "I don't remember." And neither of them can recollect. And perhaps he reads the same chapter over and over again, and they call that "studying the Bible." I do not think there is a book in the world we neglect so much as the Bible.

PROPER PASSAGES FOR FAMILY WORSHIP

Now, when you read the Bible at family worship or for private devotions, look for suitable passages. What would you think of a minister who went into the pulpit on Sunday and opened the Bible at hazard and commenced to read? Yet this is what most men do at family prayers. They might as well go into a drugstore and swallow the first medicine their eyes happen to see. Children would take more interest in family prayers if the father would take time to search for some passage to suit the special need. For instance, if any member of the family is about to travel, read Psalm 121. In time of trouble, read Psalm 91.

When the terrible accident happened to the *Spree* as we were crossing the Atlantic in November, 1892, and when none on board ship expected to live to see the light of another sun, we held a prayer meeting, at which I read a portion of Psalm 107:

> *Those who go down to the sea in ships, who do business on great waters, they see the works of the Lord, and His wonders in the deep. For He commands and raises the stormy wind, which lifts up the waves of the sea. They mount up to the heavens, they go down again to the depths; their soul melts because of trouble. They reel to and fro, and stagger like a drunken man, and are at their wits' end. Then they cry out to the Lord in their trouble, and He brings them out of their distresses. He calms the storm, so that its waves are still. Then are they glad because they are quiet; so He guides them to their desired haven. Oh, that men would give thanks*

> *to the Lord for His goodness, and for His wonderful works to the children of men!*

A lady came to me afterward and said I made it up to suit the occasion.

HELPFUL QUESTIONS FOR BIBLE STUDY

I have seen questions that will help one to get good out of every verse and passage of Scripture. They may be used in family worship, or in studying the Sabbath school lesson, or for prayer meeting, or in private reading. It would be a good thing if questions like these were pasted in the front of every Bible:

- ❖ *What persons have I read about, and what have I learned about them?*
- ❖ *What places have I read about, and what have I read about them? If the place is not mentioned, can I find out where it is? Do I know its position on the map?*
- ❖ *Does the passage refer to any particular time in the history of the children of Israel, or of some leading character?*
- ❖ *Can I tell from memory what I have just been reading?*
- ❖ *Are there any parallel passages or texts that throw light on this passage?*
- ❖ *Have I read anything about God the Father? Or about Jesus Christ? Or about the Holy Spirit?*
- ❖ *What have I read about myself? About man's sinful nature? About the spiritual new nature?*

- Is there any duty for me to observe? Any example to follow? Any promise to lay hold of? Any exhortation for my guidance? Any prayer that I may echo?
- How is this Scripture profitable for doctrine? For reproof? For correction? For instruction in righteousness?
- Does it contain the Gospel in type or in evidence?
- What is the key verse of the chapter or passage? Can I repeat it from memory?

CHAPTER SEVEN

HOW TO STUDY
THE BIBLE

NOW I WANT TO TELL YOU how I study the Bible. Every man cannot fight in Saul's armor; and perhaps you cannot follow my methods. Still, I may be able to give you some suggestions that will help. Charles Spurgeon used to prepare his sermon for Sunday morning on Saturday night. If I tried that, I would fail.

FEED YOURSELF

The quicker you learn to feed yourself, the better. I pity down deep in my heart men or women who have been attending some church or chapel for, say, five, ten, or twenty years and yet have not learned to feed themselves.

MANY . . . SIT HELPLESS AND LISTLESS, . . .
HUNGRY FOR SPIRITUAL THINGS, AND
THE MINISTER HAS TO TRY TO FEED
THEM, WHILE THE BIBLE IS A FEAST
PREPARED. . .

You know it is always regarded a great event in the family when a child can feed himself. The child is propped up at a table, and at first perhaps he uses the spoon upside down, but by and by he uses it all right, and mother, or perhaps sister, claps her hands and says, "Just see, baby's feeding himself!" Well, what we need as Christians is to be able to feed ourselves. How many there are who sit helpless and listless, with open mouths, hungry for spiritual things, and the minister has to try to feed them, while the Bible is a feast prepared, into which they never venture.

There are many who have been Christians for twenty years who have still to be fed with an ecclesiastical spoon. If they happen to have a minister who feeds them, they get on pretty well; but if they have not, they are not fed at all. This is the test as to your being a true child of God—whether you love and feed upon the Word of God. If you go out to your garden and throw down sawdust, the birds will not take any notice; but if you throw down some crumbs, you will find they will soon sweep down and pick them up. So the true child of God can tell the difference, so to speak, between sawdust and bread. Many so-called Christians are living on the world's sawdust, instead of being nourished by the Bread that comes down from heaven. Nothing can satisfy the longings of the soul but the Word of the living God.

PERSEVERE IN YOUR STUDY

The best law for Bible study is the law of perseverance. The psalmist says, "I cling to Your testimonies; O Lord" (Psalm 119:31). Application to the Word will tend to its growth within and its multiplication without. Some people are like express trains; they skim along so quickly that they see nothing.

I met a lawyer in Chicago who told me he had spent two years in studying one subject; he was trying to smash a will. He made it his business to read everything on wills he could get. Then he went into court and he talked two days about that will; he was full of it; he could not talk about anything else but wills. That is the way with the Bible—study it and study it, one subject at a time, until you become filled with it.

Read the Bible itself. Do not spend all your time on commentaries and helps. If a man spent all his time reading up the chemical constituents of bread and milk, he would soon starve.

CONSULT THREE BOOKS

For effective Bible study, there are three books which I think every Christian ought to possess.

The first, of course, is the Bible. I believe in getting a good Bible, with a good, plain print. I have not much love for those little Bibles which you have to hold right under your nose in order to read the print; and if the church happens to be a little dark, you cannot see the print, but it becomes a mere jumble of words. Someone will say, "Yes, but you cannot carry a big Bible in your pocket." Very well, then, carry it under your arm; and if you have to walk five miles, you will just be preaching a sermon five miles long. I have known a man convicted by seeing another carrying his Bible under his arm. You are not ashamed to carry hymnbooks and prayer books, and the Bible is worth all the hymnbooks and prayer books in the world put together.

If you get a good Bible, you are likely to take better care of it. Suppose you pay ten dollars for a good Bible; the older you grow, the more precious it will become to you. But be sure you do not get one so good that you will be afraid to mark it. I don't like gilt-edged Bibles that look as if they had never been used.

Next, I would advise you to get a concordance. Mine is a *Cruden's Concordance.* I was a Christian about five years before I ever heard of it. A skeptic in Boston got hold of me. I didn't know anything about the Bible, and I tried to defend the Bible and Christianity. He made a misquotation, and I said it wasn't in the Bible. I hunted for days and days. If I had had a concordance, I could have found it at once. It is a good thing for ministers once in a while to tell the people about a good book. You can find any portion or any verse in the Bible by just turning to this concordance.

Third, consult a topical textbook. These books will help you to study the Word of God with profit. If you do not possess them, get them at once; every Christian ought to have them. [One current topical textbook is *Nave's Topical Bible*, by Orville J. Nave.]

STUDY AND TEACH THE WHOLE BIBLE

I think Sunday school teachers are making a woeful mistake if they don't take the whole Bible into their Sunday school classes. I don't care how young children are; let them understand it is one book, that there are not two books: The Old Testament and the New are all one. Don't let them think that the Old Testament doesn't come to us with the same authority as the New. It is a great thing for a boy or girl to know how to handle the Bible. What is an army good for if they don't know how to handle their weapons?

I speak very strongly on this, because I know some Sabbath schools that don't have a single Bible in them. They have question books. There are questions and the answers are given just below; so that you don't need to study your lesson. They are splendid things for lazy teachers to bring along into their classes. I have seen them come into the class with a question book, and sometimes they get it wrong side up while they are talking to the class, until they find out their mistake, and then they begin over again. I have seen an examination take place something like this:

"John, who was the first man?"

"Methuselah."

"No; I think not; let me see. No, it was not Methuselah. Can't you guess again?"

"Elijah."

"No."

"Adam."

"That's right, my son; you must have studied your lesson hard."

Now, I would like to know what a boy is going to do with that kind of a teacher or with that kind of teaching. This is the kind of teaching that is worthless and brings no result. Now, don't say that I condemn helps. I believe in availing yourself of all the light you can get. What I want you to do, when you come into your classes, is to come prepared to explain the lesson without the use of a concordance. Bring the Word of God with you; bring the Old Book.

You will often find families where there is a family Bible, but the mother is so afraid that the children will tear it that she keeps it in the spare room, and once in a great while the children are allowed to look at it. The thing that interests them most is the family record—when John was born, when Father and Mother were married.

⌒

THERE IS NO PLACE IN THE WORLD THAT IS SO FASCINATING AS A LIVE BIBLE CLASS.

⌒

I came to Boston from the country and went into a Bible class where there were a few Harvard students. They handed me a Bible and told me the lesson was in John. I hunted all through the Old Testament for John but couldn't find it. I saw the fellows hunching one another, "Ah, greenie from the country." Now, you know that is just the time when you don't want to be considered green. The teacher saw my embarrassment and handed me his Bible, and I put my thumb in the place and held on. I didn't lose my place. I said then that if I ever got out of that scrape, I would never be caught there again. Why is it that so many young men from eighteen to twenty cannot be brought into a Bible class? Because they don't want to show their ignorance. There is no place in the world that is so fascinating as a live Bible class. I believe that we are to blame that they have been brought up in the Sunday school without Bibles and brought up with quarterlies instead. The result is, the boys are growing up without knowing how to handle the Bible.

Our children don't know where Matthew is; they don't know where the epistle to the Ephesians is; they don't know where to find Hebrews or any of the different books of the Bible. They ought to be taught how to handle the whole Bible, and it can be done by Sunday school teachers taking the Bible into the class and going right about it at once. You can get a Bible in this country for a small sum now. Sunday schools are not so poor that they cannot get Bibles.

⌒

A BIBLE CLASS WITHOUT A BIBLE! IT WOULD BE LIKE A DOCTOR WITHOUT A PRACTICE.

⌒

Some time ago there came up in a large Bible class a question, and they thought they would refer to the Bible, but they found that there was not a single one in the class. A Bible class without a Bible! It would be like a doctor without a practice or an army without weapons. So they went to the pews but could not find one there. Finally they went to the pulpit and took the pulpit Bible and settled the question. We are making wonderful progress, aren't we? Quarterlies are all right in their places, as helps in studying the lesson, but if they are going to sweep the Bibles out of our Sunday schools, I think we had better sweep them out.

Someone has said that there are four things necessary in studying the Bible: Admit, submit, commit, and transmit. First, admit its truth; second, submit to its teachings; third, commit it to memory; and fourth, transmit it. If the Christian life is a good thing for you, pass it on to someone else. As you study the Bible, practice those four things.

CHAPTER EIGHT

OBSERVE THE SCRIPTURES WITH A TELESCOPE

THERE ARE TWO OPPOSITE WAYS to study the Bible. One is to study it with a telescope, taking a grand sweep of a whole book and trying to find out God's plan in it; the other, with a microscope, taking up a verse at a time, dissecting it, analyzing it. If you take Genesis, it is the seed plant of the whole Bible; it tells us of *life, death,* and *resurrection;* it involves all the rest of the Bible.

We will look through the lenses of the microscope in the next chapter. Let's begin with the broad picture, to see all the distant points together. Let's first learn to look at the Scriptures with a telescope.

OBSERVING THE BIG PICTURE
IN THE BOOK OF JOB

An Englishman once remarked to me: "Mr. Moody, did you ever notice this, that the Book of Job is the key to the whole Bible? If you understand Job you will understand the entire Bible!"

"No," I said, "I don't comprehend that. Job the key to the whole Bible! How do you make that out?"

"I divide Job into seven heads," he said. "The first head is: 'A perfect man untried.' That is what God said about Job; that is Adam in Eden. He was perfect when God put him there. The second head is: 'Tried by adversity.' Job fell, as Adam fell in Eden. The third head is: 'The wisdom of the world.' The world tried to restore Job; the three wise men came to help him. That was the wisdom of the world centered in those three men. You can not," said he, "find any such eloquent language or wisdom anywhere, in any part of the world, as those three men displayed, but they did not know anything about grace, and could not, therefore, help Job."

That is just what men are trying to do; and the result is that they fail; the wisdom of man never made man any better. These three men did not help Job; they made him more unhappy. Someone has said the first man took Job and gave him a good pull; then the second and third did the same; the three of them had three good pulls at Job, and then flat down they fell.

"Then in the fourth place," said he, "'in comes the Daysman'; that is Christ. In the fifth place, 'God speaks'; and in the sixth, 'Job learns his lesson.' ('I have heard of You by the hearing of the ear, but now my eye sees You. Therefore I abhor myself, and repent in dust and ashes', Job declared in 42:5–6.) And then down came Job flat on the dunghill. The seventh head is this, that 'God restores him.'" Thank God, it is so with us, and our last state is better than our first.

That's how you observe the Scriptures with a telescope; bring all the distant points together to see the big picture. Now, let me take you through the four Gospels. Let us begin with Matthew.

OBSERVING THE BIG PICTURE IN THE GOSPEL OF MATTHEW

Christ found Matthew sitting at the receipt of custom. The Lord took someone He found at work, and he went right on working. We do not know much about what he did, except that he wrote this Gospel. But what a book! Where Matthew came from we do not know, and where he went to we do not know. His old name, Levi, dropped with his old life.

The key theme: The Messiah of the Jews and the Savior of the world. This Gospel was believed to have been written about twelve years after the death of Christ, and to be the first gospel account written. It contains the best account of the life of Christ. You notice that it is the last message of God to the Jewish nation. Here we pass from the old to the new dispensation.

A brief distinction among the four Gospels is in order. We need to see each in its place in the universe.

- ❖ *Matthew does not speak of Christ's ascension, but leaves Him on earth.*
- ❖ *Mark gives His resurrection and ascension.*
- ❖ *Luke gives His resurrection, ascension, and the promise of a Comforter.*
- ❖ *John goes a step further and says He is coming back.*

There are more quotations in Matthew than in any of the others, about one hundred. He is trying to convince the Jews that Jesus was the son of David, the rightful King. Jesus talked a good deal about the *kingdom*: its mysteries, the example of the kingdom, and so forth. The principles of the kingdom are set forth in the Sermon on the Mount. When anyone takes a kingdom, they lay down the principles upon which they are going to rule or conduct it. Matthew also presents the rejection of the King.

CHRIST USED COMMON THINGS AS ILLUSTRATIONS, AND SPOKE SO THAT EVERYONE COULD UNDERSTAND HIM.

Now, let me call your attention to five great sermons. In these you have a good sweep of the whole book:

❖ *The Sermon on the Mount. See how many things lying all around Him He brings into His sermon in Matthew 5–7. There are salt, light, candle, goat, rain, closet, moth, rust, thieves, eye, fowls, lilies, grass, dogs, bread, fish, gate, grapes, thorns, figs, thistles, rock, etc.*

Someone, in traveling through Palestine, said that he did not think there was a solitary thing there that Christ did not use as an illustration. So many people in these days are afraid to use common things, but don't you think it is better to use things that people can understand than to talk so that people can't understand you? Now a woman can easily understand a candle, and a man can easily understand about a rock, especially in a rocky country like Palestine. Christ used common things as illustrations, and spoke so that everyone could understand Him.

A woman in Wales once said she knew Christ was Welsh, and an Englishman said, "No, He was a Jew." She declared that she knew He was Welsh, because He spoke so that she could understand Him.

The Law was given on a mountain, and here Christ laid down His principles on a mountain. The Law of Moses applies to the outward acts, but this sermon applies to the inward life. As the sun is brighter than a candle, so the Sermon on the Mount is brighter than the Law of Moses. It tells us what kind of Christians we ought to be—lights in the world, the salt of the world, silent in our actions but great in effect.

❖ *The second great sermon was delivered to the twelve disciples in Matthew 10. You find over and over again the sayings in this sermon are quoted by men, such as "Shake the dust off your feet . . . against them," and "Freely you have received, freely give," etc.*

❖ *The open-air sermon. Jesus gave this sermon by the Sea of Galilee, to a great crowd (Matthew 13:1–52). You want the best kind of preaching on the street. You have to put what you say in a bright, crisp way, if you expect people to listen. This sermon contains nine parables. It is like a string of pearls. You must learn to think on your feet.*

❖ *The sermon of woes. This sermon (Matthew 23) was Christ's last appeal to the Jewish nation. Compare these eight woes with the nine Beatitudes. You notice the closing up of this sermon on woes is the most pathetic utterance in the whole ministry of Christ. "Your house is left to you desolate." Up to that time it had been "My Father's house," or "My house," but now it is "your house." It was not long until Emperor Titus came and leveled it to the ground.*

❖ *The fifth sermon was preached to His disciples (Matthew 24). How little did they understand Him! When His heart was breaking with sorrow, they drew His attention to the buildings of the temple.*

The first sermon was given on the mount; the second and third at Capernaum; the fourth in the temple; the fifth on Olivet.

In Matthew's Gospel there is not a thing in hell, heaven, earth, sea, air, or grave that does not testify of Christ as the Son of God. Devils cried out; fish entered the nets under His influence; wind and wave obeyed Him.

OBSERVING THE BIG PICTURE IN THE GOSPEL OF MARK

The four Gospels are independent of each other; not one was copied from the other. Each is the complement of the others, and we get four views of Christ, like the four sides of a house.

* *Matthew writes for Jews.*
* *Mark writes for Romans.*
* *Luke writes for Gentile converts.*
* *John writes for all who do not believe.*

You don't find any long sermons in Mark. The Romans were quick and active, and Mark had to condense things in order to catch them. In the Authorized [King James] Version, you'll find the words *forthwith, straightway,* and *immediately* occur thirty-nine times. Every chapter but the first, seventh, eighth, and fourteenth begins with "And," as if there was no pause in Christ's ministry.

HERE WE FIND THREE VERY BAD CASES—
DEVILS, DISEASE, AND DEATH—BEYOND
THE REACH OF MAN BUT CURED BY
CHRIST.

Luke tells us that Christ received little children, but Mark says He took them up in His arms. That makes it sweeter to you, doesn't it?

Perhaps the high watermark is the fifth chapter. Here we find three very bad cases—devils, disease, and death—beyond the reach of man but cured by Christ. The first man was possessed with devils. They could not bind him, chain him, or tame him. I suppose a good many men and women had been scared by that man. People are afraid of a graveyard even in daylight, but think of a live man being in the tombs and possessed with devils! He said: "What have I to do with You, Jesus, Son of the Most High God? I implore You by God that You do not torment me." But Jesus had come to do him good.

Next, the woman with the issue of blood. If she had been living today, I suppose she would have tried every patent medicine in the market. We would have declared her a hopeless case and sent her to the hospital. Someone has said: "There was more medicine in the hem of His garment than in all the apothecary shops in Palestine." She just touched Him and was made whole. Hundreds of others touched Him, but they did not get anything. Can you tell the difference between the touch of faith and the ordinary touch of the crowd?

Third, Jairus's daughter raised to life. You see the manifestation of Jesus' power is increasing, for when He arrived the child was dead and He brought her to life. I do not doubt but that away back in the secret councils of eternity it was appointed that He should be there just at that time. I remember once being called to preach a funeral sermon, and I looked the four Gospels through to find one of Christ's funeral sermons, but do you know He never preached one? He broke up every funeral He ever attended. The dead awakened when they heard His voice.

OBSERVING THE BIG PICTURE
IN THE GOSPEL OF LUKE

We now come to Luke's Gospel. You notice his name does not occur in this book or in Acts. (You will find it used three times: in Colossians, 2 Timothy, and Philemon.) He kept himself in the background. I meet numbers of Christian workers who are ruined by putting their names up. We do not know whether Luke was a Jew or Gentile.

The first we see of him is in Acts 16:10. "Now after he had seen the vision, immediately *we* sought to go to Macedonia, concluding that the Lord had called *us* to preach the gospel to them" (italics added). He did not claim to be an eyewitness to Christ's ministry nor one of the seventy. Some think he was, but he does not claim it. It is supposed that his gospel is of Paul's preaching, the same as Mark's was of Peter. It is also called the Gospel of the Gentiles, and is supposed to have been written when Paul was in Rome, perhaps between A.D. 59 and 62.

Canon Farrar has pointed out that we have a sevenfold gospel in Luke:

- ❖ *It is a gospel of praise and song. We find here the songs of Zacharias, Elizabeth, Mary, Simeon, the angels, and others. . . .*

- ❖ *It is a gospel of thanksgiving. They glorified God when Jesus healed the widow's son at Nain, when the blind man received sight, etc.*

- ❖ *It is a gospel of prayer. We learn that Christ prayed when He was baptized, and nearly every great event in His ministry was preceded by prayer. If you want to hear from heaven, you must seek it on your knees.*

- ❖ *It is a gospel of womanhood. Luke alone records many loving things Christ did for women. The richest jewel in Christ's crown was what he did for women. . . . A man once said that when God created life He began at the lowest forms of animal life and came up until He got to man, then He was not quite satisfied and created a woman. She was lifted up to the highest, and when she fell, she fell the lowest.*

❖ *This is the gospel of the poor and humble. When I get a crowd of roughs on the street, I generally teach from Luke. Here are the shepherds, the peasant, and the incident of the rich man and Lazarus. This gospel tells us He found the place where it was written, "The Spirit of the Lord is upon me . . . to preach the gospel to the poor." It is a dark day for a church when it gets out that they do not want the common people. Whitefield labored among the miners, and Wesley among the common people. If you want the poor, let it get out that you want them to come.*

❖ *It is a gospel to the lost. The woman with the seven devils, the thief on the cross illustrate this. Also, the parables of the lost sheep, the lost piece of silver, and the lost son.*

❖ *It is a gospel of tolerance. "He who wins souls is wise" (Proverbs 11:30).*

Do you want to win men? Do not drive or scold them. Do not try to tear down their prejudices before you begin to lead them to the truth. Some people think they have to tear down the scaffolding before they begin on the building. . . . Take the parable of the Good Samaritan. It has done more to stir people up to philanthropy and kindness to the poor than anything that has been said on this earth for six thousand years. Go into Samaria and you find that story has reached there first. Some man has been down to Jerusalem and heard it, and gone back home and told it all around;

and they say, "If that Prophet ever comes up here, we'll give Him a hearty reception."

If you want to reach people that do not agree with you, do not take a club to knock them down and then try to pick them up. When Jesus Christ dealt with the erring and the sinners, He was as tender with them as a mother is with her sick child.

OBSERVING THE BIG PICTURE IN THE GOSPEL OF JOHN

John was supposed to be the youngest disciple and was supposed to be the first of all that Christ had to follow Him. He is called the bosom companion of Christ. Someone was complaining of Christ's being partial. I have no doubt that Christ did love John more than the others, but it was because John loved Him most. I think John got into the inner circle, and we can get in too if we will. Christ keeps the door open and we can just go right in. You notice nearly all his book is new. All of the eight months Christ spent in Judea are recorded here.

Matthew begins with Abraham; Mark with Malachi; Luke with John the Baptist; but John with God Himself. Notice, too, these emphases among the writers of the Gospels:

❖ *Matthew sets forth Christ as the Jew's Messiah.*

❖ *Mark as the active worker.*

❖ *Luke as a man.*

❖ *John as a personal Savior.*

John presents Him as coming from the bosom of the Father. The central thought in this Gospel is proving the divinity of Christ. If I wanted to prove to a man that Jesus Christ was divine, I would take him directly to this Gospel. The word *repent* does not occur once, but the word *believe* occurs ninety-eight times. The controversy that the Jews raised about the divinity of Christ is not settled yet, and before John went away he took his pen and wrote down these things to settle it.

IF I WENT INTO COURT AND HAD SEVEN WITNESSES THAT COULD NOT BE BROKEN DOWN, I THINK I WOULD HAVE A GOOD CASE.

The Gospel According to John has a sevenfold witness to the divinity of Christ:

◈ *The testimony of the Father.* "*The Father who sent Me bears witness of Me.*"
◈ *The testimony of the Son.* "*Jesus answered and said to them, 'Even if I bear witness of Myself, my witness is true, for I know where I came from and where I am going; but you do not know where I come from and where I am going.'*"
◈ *The testimony of Christ's works.* *Jesus told the Pharisees in John* 10:37–38: "*If I do not do the works of My Father,*

do not believe Me; but if I do, though you do not believe Me, believe the works, that you may know and believe that the Father is in Me, and I in Him."

- *The testimony of the Scriptures. "For if you believed Moses, you would believe Me; for he wrote about Me."*
- *The testimony of John the Baptist. "And I have seen and testified that this is the Son of God."*
- *The testimony of the disciples. "And you also will bear witness, because you have been with Me from the beginning."*
- *The testimony of the Holy Spirit. "But when the Helper comes, whom I shall send to you from the Father, the Spirit of truth who proceeds from the Father, He will testify of Me."*

Of course, there are many others that show His divinity, but I think these are enough to prove it to any man. If I went into court and had seven witnesses that could not be broken down, I think I would have a good case.

Notice the "I am's" of Christ, another way John shows the divinity of Jesus:

- *"I am from above."*
- *"I am not of this world."*
- *"Before Abraham was, I am."*
- *"I am the bread of life."*
- *"I am the light of the world."*
- *"I am the door."*

- ❖ *"I am the good shepherd."*
- ❖ *"I am the way."*
- ❖ *"I am the truth."* Pilate asked what truth was, and there it was standing right before him.
- ❖ *"I am the resurrection and the life."*

In the gospel of John, we find eight gifts for the believer: the Bread of Life; the Water of Life; eternal life; the Holy Spirit; love; joy; peace; and His words.

CHAPTER NINE

OBSERVE THE SCRIPTURES WITH A MICROSCOPE

WE'VE BRIEFLY NOTED THAT observing the Scriptures with a microscope involves taking up a verse at a time, dissecting it, and analyzing it. Clearly that's different than the telescopic method that pulls in paragraphs and chapters at a time to grasp the larger themes.

How does the microscopic approach work? Let me show what I mean by the microscopic method by taking the first verse of Psalm 52: "Why do you boast in evil, O mighty man? The goodness of God endures continually." This verse naturally falls into two divisions: on the one side, man; on the other, God. Man—mischief; God—goodness. Is any particular man addressed? Yes: Doeg the Edomite, as the preface to the psalm suggests. You can therefore find the historic reference of this verse and psalm in 1 Samuel 22:9.

A STUDY OF *BOASTING* AND *MISCHIEF*

Now take a concordance or topical textbook, and study the subject of "boasting." What words mean the same thing as *boasting?* One is *bragging.* Is boasting always condemned? In what does Scripture forbid us to boast? In what are we exhorted to boast? God told Jeremiah, "'But let him who glories glory in this, that he understands and knows Me, that I am the Lord, exercising lovingkindness, judgment, and righteousness in the earth. For in these I delight,' says the Lord" (9:24).

Treat the subject "mischief" in a similar manner. Then ask yourself: Is this boasting, this mischief, always to last? No, "the triumphing of the wicked is short, and the joy of the hypocrite is but for a moment" (Job 20:5). David wrote in Psalm 37, "I have seen the wicked in great power, and spreading himself like a native green tree. Yet he passed away, and behold, he was no more; indeed I sought him, but he could not be found" (verses 35–36).

GOODNESS AS AN ATTRIBUTE OF GOD

The other half of the text in Psalm 52:1 suggests a study of *goodness* (or *mercy*) as an attribute of God. How is goodness manifested temporally and spiritually? What Scripture have we for it? Is God's goodness conditional? Does God's goodness conflict with His justice?

Now, as the end of Bible study as well as of preaching is to save men, ask yourself: Is the Gospel contained in this text in type or in evidence? Turn to Romans 2:4: "Or do you despise the riches of His goodness, forbearance, and longsuffering, not knowing that the goodness of God leads you to repentance?" Here the verse leads directly to the subject of repentance, and you rise from the study of the verse ready at any time to preach a short sermon that may be the means of converting someone.

The microscopic method can be used in one verse or several in a passage, but beginning a study with the telescopic method can let the student see how the specifics fit in with the general—the trees with the forest. To show this, let's change back to using a telescope for our study, as we look at Acts.

TURNING A TELESCOPE ON THE BOOK OF ACTS

A good lesson to study is how all through the book of Acts defeat was turned to victory. When the early Christians were persecuted, they went everywhere preaching the Word. That was a victory, and so on all through.

That victory can be seen by contrasting the Gospel According to Luke with Luke's Acts of the Apostles. Luke's Gospel was taken up with Christ in His body; Acts with Christ in the church. In Luke we read of what Christ did in His humiliation, and in Acts what He did in His exaltation. With most men, their work stops at their death, but with Christ it had only begun. "Greater works than these [you] will do, because I go to My Father" (John 14:12). We call this book the "Acts of the Apostles," but it is really the "Acts of the Church [Christ's body]."

You will find the key to the book in chapter 1:8: "But you shall receive power when the Holy Spirit has come upon you; and you shall be witnesses to Me in Jerusalem, and in all Judea and Samaria, and to the end of the earth."

Our microscope, focused on Acts 1:8, tells us the book is about power—spiritual power—and it comes only when the Holy Spirit comes. We see it's about a witness that will spread the church to "the end of the earth." We would not have seen the struggles of that infant church if it had not been for Luke.

There were four rivers flowing out of Eden; here we have the four Gospels flowing into one channel—the church—which is beginning, growing, and reproducing.

With our telescope, we can see the bigger picture. We can see three divisions of the Acts:

❖ *Founding of the church.*

❖ *Growth of the church.*

❖ *Sending out of missionaries.*

I believe that the nearer we keep to the apostles'

way of presenting the Gospel, the more success we will have.

TEN GREAT SERMONS

Now there are ten great sermons in Acts, and I think if you get a good hold on these you will have a pretty good understanding of the book and how to preach. Five were preached by Peter, one by Stephen, and four by Paul.

TODAY . . . WE SEEM TO BE ABOVE BEING SIMPLE WITNESSES.

The phrase, "We are witnesses," runs through the entire book and appears in these sermons. We say, today, "We are eloquent preachers." We seem to be above being simple witnesses.

Study these sermons and learn about the great themes in the book of Acts:

❖ *Peter's sermon on the Day of Pentecost. Someone said that now it takes about three thousand sermons to convert one Jew, but here three thousand, mostly Jews, were converted by one sermon. When Peter testified of Christ and bore witness that He had died and had risen again, God honored it, and He will do the same with you.*

❖ *Peter's sermon in Solomon's porch. A short sermon, but it* did good work. Peter and John did not get there till three o'clock, and I believe the Jews could not arrest a man after sundown, and yet in that short space of time five thousand were converted. What did he preach? The heart of his message was: "But you . . . killed the Prince of Life, whom God raised from the dead, of which we are witnesses. . . . Repent therefore and be converted, that your sins may be blotted out, so that times of refreshing may come from the presence of the Lord." (See Acts 3:12–4:4.)

❖ Peter's sermon to the high priest and Jewish religious leaders. They had arrested them and were demanding to know by what power they did these things. "By the name of Jesus Christ . . . this man stands here before you whole," Peter said in his sermon (Acts 4:10; see 4:5–12).

❖ Peter and John's testimony before the council. The council commanded the two not to preach in the name of Christ. Peter and John's mini-sermon, only two sentences, was a bold response declaring "we cannot but speak the things which we have seen and heard" (Acts 4:20; see 4:15–22). About all the disciples knew was what they had learned in those three years with Jesus, hearing His sermons and seeing His miracles. They saw the things and knew they were so, and when the Holy Ghost came down upon them, they could not help but speak them.

❖ Stephen's sermon. He preached the longest sermon in Acts (see 7:2–53). Dr. Bonar once said, "Did you ever notice,

Brother Whittle, that when the Jews accused Stephen of speaking blasphemous words against Moses, the Lord lit up his face with the same glory with which Moses' face shone?"

❖ Peter's last sermon and the first sermon to the Gentiles. Notice the same Gospel was preached to the Gentiles as to the Jews, and it produced the same results. "To Him all the prophets witness that, through His name, whoever believes in Him will receive remission of sins." (10:43; see 10:24–43).

Now the leading character changes, and Paul comes on.

❖ Paul's sermon at Antioch, in Pisidia. "Therefore let it be known to you, brethren, that through this Man is preached to you the forgiveness of sins" (13:38; see 14–41). If you want to get people to come to hear you, lift up Christ; He said, "I, if I be lifted up from the earth, will draw all peoples to Myself."

❖ Paul's sermon to the Athenians. He got fruit at Athens by preaching the same old Gospel to the philosophers (see 17:18–34).

❖ Paul's sermon at Jerusalem (see 22:1–24).

❖ Paul's defense before Agrippa in Acts 26. I think that is the grandest sermon Paul ever preached. He preached the same Gospel before Agrippa and Festus that he did down *in Jerusalem. He preached everywhere the mighty fact that God gave Christ as a ransom for sin, that the whole world can be saved by trusting in Him.*

The theme of being witnesses reappears in this great sermon. "Therefore, having obtained help from God, to this day I stand, witnessing both to small and great, saying no other things than those which the prophets and Moses said would come—that the Christ would suffer, that He would be the first to rise from the dead, and would proclaim light to the Jewish people and to the Gentiles" (26:22–23).

CHAPTER TEN

⟨ornament⟩

SURVEYING A BIBLE BOOK

I KNOW SOME MEN WHO NEVER sit down to read a book until they have time to read the whole of it. When they come to Leviticus or Numbers, or any one of the other books, they read it right through at one sitting. They get the whole sweep, and then they begin to study it chapter by chapter. Dean Stanley used to read a book through three separate times: first for the story, second for the thought, and third for the literary style. It is a good thing to take one whole book at a time.

How could you expect to understand a story or a scientific textbook if you read one chapter here and another there?

FINDING THE PURPOSE AND POINTS OF A BIBLE BOOK

Dr. A. T. Pierson says, "Let the introduction cover five P's: place where written, person by whom written, people to whom written, purpose for which written, and period at which written." Those are the first steps in surveying a Bible book.

> "TELL ME FROM MEMORY WHAT YOU FIND IN THAT CHAPTER AND . . . LEARN THE VERSE IN IT THAT IS MOST PRE-CIOUS TO YOU."

Here it is well to grasp the leading points in the chapters. The method of surveying a Bible book is illustrated by the following plan by which I tried to interest the students at the Mt. Hermon school and the Northfield Seminary. It provides a way of committing Scripture to memory, so that one can call up a passage to meet the demand whenever it arises.

I said to the students one morning at worship: "Tomorrow morning when I come I will not read a portion of Scripture, but we will take the first chapter of the Gospel of John and you shall tell me from memory what you find in that chapter and each shall learn the verse in it that is most precious to you." We went through the whole book that way and committed a verse or two to memory out of each chapter.

THE GOSPEL OF JOHN, BY CHAPTERS

I will give the main headings, key words, and memory verses that we chose for the twenty-one chapters of the Gospel According to John.

* Chapter 1. The call of the first five disciples. *It was about four o'clock in the afternoon that John stood and said, "Behold! The Lamb of God who takes away the sin of the world!" (verse 29). Two of John's disciples then followed Jesus; and one of them, Andrew, went out and brought his brother Simon. Then Jesus found Philip, as He was starting for Galilee, and Philip found Nathanael, the skeptical man. When he got sight of Christ, his skeptical ideas were all gone. The key word is* receiving. *Commit to memory verses 11 and 12: "He came to His own, and His own did not receive Him. But as many as received Him, to them He gave the right to become children of God, even to those who believe in His name."*

* Chapter 2. Obedience. *The key word in this chapter is* obedience, *and the key verse to memorize is verse 5: "Whatever He says to you, do it."*

* Chapter 3. Regeneration. *It took us more than one day to get through John 3. This chapter presents a respectable sinner and how Jesus dealt with him. The key word is* believing. *Commit to memory verse 16: "God so*

109

loved the world that He gave His only begotten Son, that whoever believes in Him should not perish but have everlasting life."

❖ Chapter 4. A disreputable sinner and how Jesus dealt with her. *If we had been dealing with the Samaritan woman, we would have told her what Jesus told Nicodemus, but He took her on her own ground. She came for a pot of water, and, thank God, she got a whole well full. The key word is* worshiping. *Memorize verse 24: "God is Spirit, and those who worship Him must worship in spirit and truth."*

⌒

IF YOU WANT A GOOD LOAF OF BREAD, GET INTO JOHN'S SIXTH CHAPTER.

⌒

❖ Chapter 5. The divinity of Christ. *The key word is* healing. *Commit to memory verse 24: "Most assuredly, I say to you, he who hears My word and believes in Him who sent Me has everlasting life, and shall not come into judgment, but has passed from death into life."*

❖ Chapter 6. Christ, the Bread of Life. *If you want a good loaf of bread, get into John's sixth chapter. You feed upon that Bread and you will live forever. The key word is* eating. *Commit to memory verse 51: "I am the living bread which came down from heaven. If anyone eats of* this bread, he will live forever; and the bread that I shall give is My flesh, which I shall give for the life of the world."

❖ Chapter 7. Water. *You have here living water and Christ's invitation to every thirsty soul to come to drink. The key word is* drinking. *The key verse to memorize is verse 37: "If anyone thirsts, let him come to Me and drink."*

❖ Chapter 8. Light. *The key phrase is* walking in the light. *Commit to memory verse 12: "I am the light of the world." But what is the use of having light if you have no eyes to see with, so we go to chapter 9, the sight chapter.*

❖ Chapter 9. Sight. *There was a man born blind and Christ made him to see. The key word is* testifying. *A key verse to memorize is verse 4: "I must work the works of Him who sent Me while it is day; the night is coming when no one can work."*

❖ Chapter 10. The Good Shepherd. *The key word is* safety. *Commit to memory verse 11: "I am the good shepherd. The good shepherd gives His life for the sheep."*

❖ Chapter 11. Lazarus. *The key word is* resurrection. *Memorize verse 25: "I am the resurrection and the life. He who believes in Me, though he may die, he shall live."*

❖ Chapter 12. Salvation. *Here Christ closes up His ministry to the Jewish nation. The key word is* salvation, *and the key verse is verse 32: "And I, if I am lifted up from the earth, will draw all peoples to Myself."*

❖ Chapter 13. Humility. *In this chapter, Christ washes the feet of His disciples. The key word is* teaching, *and the key verse is verse 34:* "A new commandment I give to you, that you love one another."

❖ Chapter 14. Mansion. *The key words are* peace *and* comfort. *Commit to memory verse 6:* "I am the way, the truth, and the life. No one comes to the Father except through Me."

❖ Chapter 15. Fruit. *The vine can only bear fruit through the branches. The key word is* joy. *Commit to memory verse 5:* "I am the vine, you are the branches. He who abides in Me, and I in him, bears much fruit; for without Me you can do nothing."

❖ Chapter 16. The promise of the Holy Sprit. *Here you find the secret of power.* Power *is the key word. Commit to memory verse 8:* "And when He [the Holy Spirit] has come, He will convict the world of sin, and of righteousness, and of judgment."

❖ Chapter 17. Intercession. *This chapter contains what is properly called the "Lord's prayer," prayed on behalf of all followers of Christ. The key word is* separation. *Commit to memory verse 15:* "I do not pray that You should take them out of the world, but that You should keep them from the evil one."

❖ Chapter 18. Arrest. *Christ is arrested.*

❖ Chapter 19. Crucifixion. *Christ is crucified.*

CHAPTER ELEVEN

STUDYING BIBLE TYPES AND BIBLE CHARACTERS

LET'S LOOK AT TWO KINDS of Bible studies. The first is a study of types in the Bible; the second is a study of specific people whose stories appear in the Scriptures. Each method can be a profitable way to study the Scriptures.

The Bible is full of patterns and types of ourselves. One popular objection against the Bible is that those types tell about the failings of men. We should, however, remember that the object of the Bible is not to tell how good men are, but how bad men can become good. But more especially the Bible is full of types of Christ.

Both patterns reveal truths about God and ourselves. Types are foreshadowings, and wherever there is a shadow, there must be a substance. God seems to have chosen this means of teaching the Israelites of the promised Messiah. All the laws, ceremonies, and institutions of the Mosaic dispensation point to Christ and His dispensation.

TYPES IN THE TABERNACLE

The enlightened eyes see Christ in all, because types typically foreshadow—or prefigure—Christ. For instance, the tabernacle was a type of the incarnation of Jesus: John wrote, "And the Word became flesh and dwelt"—the word means tabernacled—"among us" (1:14).

Several items in the Tabernacle typified Christ or His future ministry. The laver typified sanctification or purity: "that He might sanctify and cleanse her [the church] with the washing of water by the word" (Ephesians 5:26). The candlesticks typified Christ as the Light of the World. The showbread typified Christ as the Bread of Life. The high priest was also a type of Christ. Christ was called of God, as was Aaron; "He always lives to make intercession for them" (Hebrews 7:25); He was consecrated with an oath, and so on.

The Passover, the Day of Atonement, the smitten rock, the sacrifices, the city of refuge, the brazen serpent—all point to Christ's atoning work.

TYPES FROM ADAM TO JOSEPH

Adam was a beautiful type. Think of the two Adams. One introduced sin and ruin into the world; the other came to abolish it. So Cain stands as the representative natural man, and Abel as the spiritual man. Abel as a shepherd is a type of Christ the heavenly Shepherd.

A COMPARISON OF THE LIVES OF JOSEPH AND JESUS SHOWS A STARTLING SIMILARITY IN THEIR EXPERIENCES.

There is no more beautiful type of Christ in the Bible than Joseph. He was hated of his brethren; he was stripped of his coat; he was sold; he was imprisoned; he gained favor; he had a gold chain about his neck. Eventually, every knee bowed before him. A comparison of the lives of Joseph and Jesus shows a startling similarity in their experiences.

From Adam to Joseph, several of the patriarchs represent important biblical concepts:

- *Adam represents man's innate sinfulness.*
- *Abel represents atonement.*
- *Enoch represents communion.*
- *Noah represents regeneration.*

❖ *Abraham represents faith.*

❖ *Isaac represents sonship.*

❖ *Jacob represents discipline and service.*

❖ *Joseph represents glory through suffering.*

The disease of leprosy represents a type of sin. It works baneful results; it is insidious in its nature, and from a small beginning works complete ruin. It separates its victims from their fellowmen, just as sin separates a man from God. And as Christ had power to cleanse the leper, so by the grace of God His blood cleanses us from all iniquity.

PEOPLE OF THE BIBLE

Another good way is to study Bible characters—take them right from the cradle to the grave. You find that skeptics often take one particular part of a man's life—say, of the life of Jacob or of David—and judge the whole by that. They say that these men were strange saints; and yet God did not punish them. If you go right through these men's lives, you will find that God did punish them, according to the sins they committed.

A lady once said to me that she had trouble in reading the Bible, that she seemed to not feel the interest she ought. Read about flesh-and-blood people, and you will have interest.

If you don't keep up your interest in one way, try another. Never think you have to read the Bible by courses.

PERSONAL NAMES

As you study Bible characters, consider a smaller but still interesting study . . . the meaning of proper names. I need hardly remark that every name in the Bible, especially Hebrew names, has a meaning of its own. Notice the difference between Abram ("a high father"), and Abraham ("father of a multitude"), and you have a key to his life. Another example is Jacob. Originally named Jacob, or "supplanter," God renamed him Israel, meaning "Prince of God."

THE NAMES OF HIS DAUGHTERS SIGNI-
FIED BEAUTY, SO THAT JOB'S LEPROSY
LEFT NO TAINT.

Finally, think of the names of Job's three daughters. They were Jemima, meaning "a dove"; Kezia, meaning "cassia," a fragrant cinnamon bark; and Keren-happuch, meaning "horn of paint." The names of his daughters signified beauty, so that Job's leprosy ("boils") left no taint.

CHAPTER TWELVE

STUDYING GREAT BIBLE DOCTRINES AND TOPICS

NOW AND THEN I MEET some people who boast that they have read the Bible through in so many months. Others read the Bible chapter by chapter, and get through it in a year; but I think it would be almost better to spend a year over one book. If I went into a court of justice and wanted to carry the jury with me, I should get every witness I could to testify to the one point on which I wanted to convince the jury. I would not get them to testify to everything, but just to that one thing. And so it should be with the Scriptures.

Once, I took up the word *love,* and I do not know how many weeks I spent in studying the passages in which it occurs, till at last I could not help loving people. I had been feeding so long on love that I was anxious to do good to everyone I came in contact with.

Take *sanctification*. I would rather take my concordance and gather passages on sanctification and sit down for four or five days and study them than have men tell me about it.

THREE GREAT DOCTRINES: FAITH, JUSTIFICATION, AND ATONEMENT

I suppose that if all the time that I have prayed for *faith* were put together, it would be months. I used to say when I was president of the Young Men's Christian Association in Chicago, "What we want is faith. If we have only faith, we can turn Chicago upside down"— or rather, right side up. I thought that someday faith was going to come down and strike me like lightning. But faith did not seem to come. One day I read in the tenth chapter of Romans, "Faith comes by hearing, and hearing by the word of God." I had closed my Bible, and prayed for faith. I now opened my Bible, and began to study, and faith has been growing ever since.

Take the doctrine that made Martin Luther such a power, *justification*. "The just shall live by faith." When that thought flashed through Martin Luther's mind as he was ascending the Scala Santa on his knees (although some people deny the truth of this statement), he rose and went forth to be a power among the nations of the earth. Justification puts a man before God as if he had never sinned; he stands before God like Jesus Christ. Thank God, in Jesus Christ we can be perfect, but there is no perfection out of Him. God looks in His ledger and says, "Moody, your debts have all been paid by Another; there is nothing against you."

THE ATONEMENT IS FORESHADOWED IN THE GARDEN OF EDEN . . . [IN] THE ANIMALS SLAIN FOR ADAM'S SIN.

In New England there is perhaps no doctrine assailed so much as the *Atonement*. The Atonement is foreshadowed in the garden of Eden; there is the innocent suffering for the guilty, the animals slain for Adam's sin. We find it in Abraham's day, in Moses' day; all through the Books of Moses and the prophets.

The Atonement is in the Old and New Testaments. Look at Isaiah 53 and at the prophecy of Daniel. Then we come into the Gospels, and Christ says, "I lay down My life that I may take it again. No one takes it from Me, but I lay it down of Myself."

A STUDY OF CONVERSION

People talk about *conversion*—what is conversion? The best way to find out is from the Bible. A good many don't believe in sudden conversions. You can die in a moment. Can't you receive life in a moment?

When Ira Sankey and myself were in one place in Europe, a man preached a sermon against the "pernicious" doctrines that we were going to preach, one of which was sudden conversion. He said conversion was a matter of time and growth. Do you know what I do when any man preaches against the doctrines I preach? I go to the Bible and find out what it says, and if I am right, I give them more of the same kind. I preached more on sudden conversion in that town than in any town I was in in my life.

I would like to know how long it took the Lord to convert Zaccheus? How long did it take the Lord to convert that woman whom He met at the well of Sychar? How long to convert that adulterous woman in the temple, who was caught in the very act of adultery? How long to convert that woman who anointed His feet and wiped them with the hairs of her head? Didn't she go with the word of God's Son ringing in her ears, "Go in peace"?

There was no sign of Zaccheus being converted when he went up that sycamore tree, and he was converted when he came down, so he must have been converted between the branch and the ground. Pretty sudden work, wasn't it? But you say, "That is because Christ was there." Friends, they were converted a good deal faster after He went away than when He was here. Peter preached, and three thousand were converted in one day. Another time, after three o'clock in the afternoon, Peter and John healed a man at the gate of the Temple and then went in and preached, and five thousand were added to the church before night, and they were Jews. That was rather sudden work.

Professor Drummond describes a man going into one of our after-meetings and saying he wanted to become a Christian. "Well, my friend, what is the trouble?" He didn't like to tell. He was greatly agitated. Finally he said, "The fact is, I have overdrawn my account"—a polite way of saying he had been stealing.

"Did you take your employer's money?"

"Yes."

"How much?"

"I don't know. I never kept account of it."

"Well, you have an idea that you stole $1,500 last year?"

"I am afraid it is that much."

"Now, look here, sir, I don't believe in sudden work; don't you steal more than a thousand dollars this next year, and the next year not more than five hundred, and in the course of the next few years you will get so that you won't steal any by and by."

My friends, the thing is a perfect farce. "Let him that stole steal no more," that is what the Bible says. It is right about-face.

Take another illustration. Here comes a man and he admits that he gets drunk every week. That man comes to a meeting and he wants to be converted. I say, "Don't you be in a hurry. I believe in doing the work gradually. Don't you get drunk and knock your wife down more than once a month. Wouldn't it be refreshing to your wife to go a whole month without being knocked down? Once a month, only twelve times in a year! Wouldn't she be glad to have you converted in this new way! Only get drunk after a few years on the anniversary of your wedding, and at Christmas; and then it will be effective because it is gradual." Oh! I detest all that kind of teaching. Let us go to the Bible and see what that old Book teaches. Let us believe it, and go and act as if we believed it, too.

I BELIEVE A MAN MAY BE AS VILE AS HELL IT-
SELF ONE MOMENT AND BE SAVED THE NEXT.

Salvation is instantaneous. I admit that a man may be converted so that he cannot tell when he crossed the line between death and life, but I also believe a man may be a thief one moment and a saint the next. I believe a man may be as vile as hell itself one moment and be saved the next.

Christian growth is gradual, just as physical growth is; but a man passes from death unto everlasting life quick as an act of the mind—"He who believes in the Son has everlasting life."

ABOUT HEAVEN . . . ABOUT REVIVAL

People say they want to become heavenly minded.

Well, read about heaven and talk about it. I once preached on heaven, and after the meeting a lady came to me and said, "Why, Mr. Moody, I didn't know there were so many verses in the Bible about heaven." And I hadn't taken one out of a hundred. She was amazed that there was so much in the Bible about heaven.

When you are away from home, how you look for news! You skip everything in the daily paper until your eye catches the name of your own town or country. Now the Christian's home is in heaven. The Scriptures contain our title deeds to everything we shall be worth when we die. If a will has your name in it, it is no longer a dry document. Why, then, do not Christians take more interest in the Bible?

SPEND A MONTH ON *REGENERATION*, OR *THE KINGDOM OF GOD*, . . . OR *THE ATTRIBUTES OF GOD*. IT WILL HELP YOU IN YOUR OWN SPIRITUAL LIFE.

Then, again, people say they don't believe in *revivals*. There's not a denomination in the world that didn't spring from a revival. There are the Catholic and Episcopal churches claiming to be the apostolic churches and to have sprung from Pentecost; the Lutheran from Martin Luther, and so on. They all sprang out of revivals, and yet people talk against revivals! Wasn't the country revived under John the Baptist? Wasn't it under Christ's teachings?

People think that because a number of superficial cases of conversion occur at revivals that therefore revivals ought to be avoided. They forget the parable of the sower, where Jesus Himself warned us of emotional hearers, who receive the word with joy, but soon fall away. If only one out of every four hearers is truly converted, as in the parable, the revival has done good.

Suppose you spend a month on *regeneration,* or *the kingdom of God,* or *the church,* or the *divinity of Christ* or the *attributes of God.* It will help you in your own spiritual life, and you will become a workman who needs not be ashamed, rightly dividing the Word of Truth.

MORE WORD STUDIES

Make a study of the *Holy Spirit.* There are probably five hundred passages on the Holy Spirit, and what you want is to study this subject for yourself.

Take *the return of our Lord.* I know it is a controverted subject. Some say He is to come at the end of the millennium; others say this side of the millennium. What we want is to know what the Bible says. Why not go to the Bible and study it for yourself; it will be worth more to you than anything you get from anyone else.

Then there is *separation.* I believe that a Christian man and woman should lead separated lives. The line between the church and the world is almost obliterated today. I have no sympathy with the idea that you must hunt up an old musty church record in order to find out whether a man is a member of the church or not. A man ought to live so that everybody will know he is a Christian.

The Bible tells us to lead separate lives. We may lose influence, but we will gain it at the same time. I suppose Daniel was the most unpopular man in Babylon at a certain time, but, thank God, he outlived all the other men of his time. Who were the chief men of Babylon? When God wanted any work done in Babylon, He knew where to find someone to do it. You can be in the world, but not of it. Christ didn't take His disciples out of the world, but He prayed that they might be kept from evil. A ship in the water is all right, but when the water gets into the ship, then look out. A worldly Christian is just like a tossed vessel at sea.

I remember once I took up the *grace of God*. I didn't know the difference between law and grace. When that truth dawned upon me and I saw the difference, I studied the whole week on grace, and I got so filled that I couldn't stay in the house. I said to the first man I met, "Do you know anything about the grace of God?" He thought I was a lunatic. And I just poured out for about an hour on the grace of God.

Study the subject of *prayer*. "For real business at the mercy seat," says Spurgeon, "give me a home-made prayer, a prayer that comes out of the depths of your heart, not because you invented it, but because the Holy

Spirit put it there. Though your words are broken and your sentences disconnected, God will hear you. Perhaps you can pray better without words than with them. There are prayers that break the backs of words; they are too heavy for any human language to carry."

ASSURANCE AND THE PROMISES OF GOD

Some people say, "I do not believe in *assurance*." I never knew anybody who read their Bibles who did not believe in assurance. This Book teaches nothing else. Paul says, "I know whom I have believed." Job says, "I know that my Redeemer lives." It is not "I hope." It's "I trust."

The best book on assurance was written by the disciple called John, at the back part of the Bible. He wrote an epistle on this subject. Sometimes you just get a word that will be a sort of key to the epistle, and which unfolds it. Now if you turn to John 20:31, you will find it says, "These are written that you may believe that Jesus is the Christ, the Son of God, and that believing you may have life in His name." Then if you turn to 1 John 5:13, you will read: "These things I have written to you who believe in the name of the Son of God, that you may *know* that you have eternal life, and that you may continue to believe in the name of the Son of God" (italics added).

That whole epistle is written on assurance. I have no doubt John had found some people who questioned their assurance and doubted whether they were saved. He took up his pen and said, "I will settle that question;" and he wrote that last verse in the twentieth chapter of his gospel.

I have heard some people say that it was not their privilege to know that they were saved; they had heard the minister say that no one could know whether he were saved or not; and they took what the minister said, instead of what the Word of God said. Others read the Bible to make it fit in and prove their favorite creed or notions; and if it does not do so, they will not read it.

It has been well said that we must not read the Bible by the blue light of Presbyterianism; nor by the red light of Methodism; nor by the violet light of Episcopalianism; but by the light of the Spirit of God. If you will take up your Bible and study "assurance" for a week, you will soon see it is your privilege to know that you are a child of God.

IF YOU WOULD SPEND A MONTH FEEDING ON THE PRECIOUS PROMISES OF GOD, YOU WOULD NOT GO ABOUT WITH YOUR HEAD HANGING DOWN.

Then take the *promises of God*. Let a man feed for a month on the promises of God, and he will not talk about his poverty, and how downcast he is, and what trouble he has day by day. You hear people say, "Oh, my leanness! How lean I am!" My friends, it is not their leanness, it is their *laziness*. If you would only go from Genesis to Revelation, and see all the promises made by God to Abraham, to Isaac, and to Jacob, to the Jews and the Gentiles, and to all His people everywhere. If you would spend a month feeding on the precious promises of God, you would not go about with your heads hanging down like bulrushes, complaining how poor you are; but you would lift up your heads with confidence and proclaim the riches of His grace, because you could not help it.

After the Chicago Fire, a man came up to me and said in a sympathizing tone, "I understand you lost everything, Moody, in the Chicago fire."

"Well, then," said I, "someone has misinformed you."

"Indeed! Why, I was told certainly you had lost all. Have you got much left, then?" asked my friend.

"Yes," I replied, "I have got much more left than I lost; though I cannot tell how much I have lost."

"Well, I am glad of it, Moody; I did not know you were that rich before the fire."

"Yes," said I, "I am a good deal richer than you could conceive; and here is my title deed, 'He who overcomes shall inherit all things'" (Revelation 21:7).

They say the Rothschilds cannot tell how much they are worth; and that is just my case. All things in the world are mine; I am a joint heir with Jesus the Son of God. Someone has said, "God makes a promise. Faith believes it; hope anticipates it; and patience quietly awaits it."

CHAPTER THIRTEEN

WORD STUDIES AND A SUMMARY OF SUGGESTED METHODS

ANOTHER WAY TO STUDY THE BIBLE is to take one word and follow it through all the Scriptures with the help of a concordance.

Or take just one word that runs through a book. Some time ago I was wonderfully blessed by taking the seven *blesseds* of the Revelation. If God did not wish us to understand the book of Revelation, He would not have given it to us at all. A good many say it is so dark and mysterious that common readers cannot understand it. Let us only keep digging away at it, and it will unfold itself by and by. Someone says it is the only book in the Bible that tells about the devil being chained; and as the devil knows that, he goes up and down

Christendom and says, "It is no use reading Revelation; you cannot understand the book; it is too hard for you." The fact is, he does not want you to understand about his defeat.

THE SEVEN "BLESSEDS" OF REVELATION

Just look at those seven blessings contained in the book of Revelation:

- ❖ *"Blessed is he who reads and those who hear the words of this prophecy, and keep those things which are written in it; for the time is near"* (1:3).
- ❖ *"'Blessed are the dead who die in the Lord' . . . . 'Yes,' says the Spirit, 'that they may rest from their labors'"* (14:13).
- ❖ *"Blessed is he who watches, and keeps his garments"* (16:15).
- ❖ *"'Blessed are those who are called to the marriage supper of the Lamb!'"* (19:9).
- ❖ *"Blessed and holy is he who has part in the first resurrection. Over such the second death has no power, but they shall be priests of God and of Christ, and shall reign with Him a thousand years"* (20:6).
- ❖ *"Blessed is he who keeps the words of the prophecy of this book"* (22:7).
- ❖ *"Blessed are those who do His commandments, that they may have the right to the tree of life, and may enter through the gates into the city"* (22:14).

Or you may take the eight *"overcomes"* in Revelation; and you will be wonderfully blessed by them. They take you right up to the throne of heaven; you climb by them to the throne of God.

I have been greatly blessed by going through the *"believings"* of John. Every chapter but two speaks of believing. As I said before, he wrote his gospel that we might believe. All through it is "Believe! *Believe!*" If you want to persuade a man that Christ is the Son of God, John's Gospel is the book for him.

Take the six *"precious"* things in Peter's epistles. And the seven *"walks"* of the epistle to the Ephesians. And the five *"much mores"* of Romans 5. Or the two *"receiveds"* of John 1. Or the seven *"hearts"* in Proverbs 23, and especially an eighth.

LEARNING ABOUT "THE FEAR OF THE LORD"

You can learn much about *the fear of the Lord* by studying the phrase in Proverbs:

- ❖ *"The fear of the Lord is the beginning of wisdom"* (9:10).
- ❖ *"The fear of the Lord is to hate evil"* (8:13).
- ❖ *"The fear of the Lord prolongs days"* (10:27).
- ❖ *"In the fear of the Lord there is strong confidence"* (14:26).
- ❖ *"The fear of the Lord is a fountain of life"* (14:27).
- ❖ *"Better is a little with the fear of the Lord, than great treasure with trouble"* (15:16).

- ❖ *"The fear of the Lord is the instruction of wisdom"* (15:33).
- ❖ *"By the fear of the Lord one departs from evil"* (16:6).
- ❖ *"The fear of the Lord leads to life"* (19:23).
- ❖ *"By humility and the fear of the Lord are riches and honor and life"* (22:4).
- ❖ *"Be zealous in the fear of the Lord all the day"* (23:17).

KEY WORDS IN THE NEW TESTAMENT BOOKS

A friend gave me some key words. He said Peter wrote about *hope:* "When the Chief Shepherd appears." The keynote of Paul's writings seemed to be *faith,* and that of John's, *love.* "Faith, hope, and love"; those were the characteristics of the three men, the keynotes to the whole of their teachings. James wrote of *good works,* and Jude of *apostasy.*

In the general epistles of Paul, someone has suggested the phrase *in Christ.* In the book of Romans we find justification by faith *in Christ.* Corinthians presents sanctification *in Christ.* The book of Galatians is about adoption or liberty *in Christ.* Ephesians presents fullness *in Christ.* Philippians, consolation *in Christ.* In Colossians we have completeness *in Christ.* First Thessalonians gives us hope *in Christ.*

Different systems of key words are published by Bible scholars, and it is a good thing for everyone to know one system.

A SUMMARY OF SUGGESTIONS

Word studies are only one of several ways to study the Bible for pleasure and profit. Here is a summary of suggestions for effective Bible study based on what we've learned so far, as well as several other ideas.

1. Have for constant use a portable reference Bible, a concordance, and a topical textbook.
2. Set apart at least fifteen minutes a day for study and meditation. This little time will have great results and will never be regretted.
3. Prepare your heart to know the law of the Lord, and *to do it* (see Ezra 7:10).
4. Always ask God to open the eyes of your understanding that you may see the truth; and expect that He will answer your prayer.
5. Cast every burden of doubt upon the Lord. "He shall sustain you; He shall never permit the righteous to be moved." Do not be afraid to look for a reason for the hope that is in you.
6. Believe in the Bible as God's revelation to you, and act accordingly. Do not reject any portion because it contains the supernatural or because you cannot understand it. Reverence all Scripture. Remember God's own estimate of it: "You have magnified Your word above all Your name" (Psalm 138:2).

7. Learn at least one verse of Scripture each day. Verses committed to memory will be wonderfully useful in your daily life and walk. "Your word I have hidden in my heart, that I might not sin against You." (Psalm 119:11). Some Christians can quote Shakespeare and Longfellow better than the Bible.

8. If you are a preacher or a Sunday school teacher, try at any cost to master your Bible. You ought to know it better than anyone in your congregation or class.

9. Strive to be exact in quoting Scripture.

10. Always carry a Bible or New Testament in your pocket, and do not be ashamed of people seeing you read it on trains, buses, and so on.

11. Do not be afraid of marking your Bible or of making marginal notes. (We will look at this approach in depth in the next chapter.) Mark texts that contain promises, exhortations, warnings to sinners and to Christians, gospel invitations to the unconverted, and so on.

12. Adopt some systematic plan of Bible study; either topical, or by subjects, like "the blood," "prayer," "hope," etc., or by books; or by some other plan outlined in the preceding pages.

13. Study to know for what and to whom each book of the Bible was written. Combine the Old Testament with the New. Study Hebrews and Leviticus together, the Acts of the Apostles and the

Pauline Epistles, the Minor Prophets and the Historical Books of the Old Testament.

14. Study how to use the Bible so as to "walk with God" in closer communion; also, so as to gain a working knowledge of Scripture for leading others to Christ.

15. Do not be satisfied with simply reading a chapter daily. Study the meaning of at least one verse.

CHAPTER FOURTEEN

MARKING YOUR BIBLE

AN OLD WRITER SAID THAT some books are to be tasted, some to be swallowed, and some to be chewed and digested. The Bible is one that you can never exhaust. It is like a bottomless well: You can always find fresh truths gushing forth from its pages.

Hence the great fascination of constant and earnest Bible study. Hence also the necessity of marking your Bible. Unless you have uncommon memory, you cannot retain the good things you hear. If you trust to your ear alone, they will escape you in a day or two; but if you mark your Bible and enlist the aid of your eye, you will never lose them. The same applies to what you read.

THE BENEFITS OF BIBLE MARKING

Bible marking should be made the servant of a person's memory. If properly done, it sharpens the memory rather than blunts it, because it gives prominence to certain things that catch the eye, which by constant reading you get to learn by heart.

It helps you to locate texts.

It saves you the trouble of writing out notes of your addresses. Once in the margin, it's always ready.

I have carried one Bible with me a great many years. It is worth a good deal to me, and I will tell you why: I have so many passages marked in it, that if called upon to speak at any time I am ready. I have little words marked in the margin, and they are a sermon to me. Whether I speak about faith, hope, love, assurance, or any subject whatever, it all comes back to me; and however unexpectedly I am called upon to preach, I am always ready. Every child of God ought to be like a soldier, and always hold himself in readiness. If men of England's army were ordered to India tomorrow, the soldier is ready for the journey. But we cannot be ready if we do not study the Bible.

So whenever you hear a good thing, just put it down, because if it is good for you it will be good for somebody else; and we should pass the coin of heaven around just as we do the coin of our realm.

People tell me they have nothing to say. "Out of the abundance of the heart the mouth speaks." Get full of Scripture and then you can't help but say it; it says itself. Keep the world out of your heart by getting full of something else.

A man tried to build a flying machine. He made some wings and filled them with a gas. He said he couldn't quite fly, but the gas was lighter than the air and it helped him over lots of obstructions. So when you get these heavenly truths, they are lighter than the air down there and help you rise over trouble.

Bible marking makes the Bible a new book to you. If there was a white birch tree within a quarter of a mile of the home of your boyhood, you would remember it all your life. Mark your Bible, and instead of its being dry and uninteresting, it will become a beautiful Book to you. What you see makes a more lasting impression on your memory than what you hear.

HOW TO MARK AND WHAT TO MARK

There are many methods of marking. Some use six or eight colored inks or pencils. Black is used to mark texts that refer to sin; red, all references to the Cross; blue, all references to heaven; and so on. Others invent symbols. When there is any reference to the cross, they put † in the margin. Some write G, meaning the Gospel.

There is a danger of overdoing this and making your marks more prominent than the Scripture itself. If the system is complicated, it becomes a burden, and you are likely to be confused. It is easier to remember the text than the meaning of your marks.

Black ink is good enough for all purposes. I use no other, unless it be red ink to draw attention to "the blood."

WHEN ANY WORD OR PHRASE IS OFT
REPEATED IN A CHAPTER OR BOOK, PUT
CONSECUTIVE NUMBERS IN THE MARGIN.

The simplest way to mark is to underline the words or to make a stroke alongside the verse. Another good way is to go over the printed letters with your pen, and make them thicker. The word will then stand out like heavier type. Mark "only" in Psalm 62 this way.

When any word or phrase is oft repeated in a chapter or book, put consecutive numbers in the margin over against the text. Thus, in the second chapter of Habakkuk, we find five "woes" against five common sins: (1) verse 6, (2) verse 9, (3) verse 12, (4) verse 15, and (5) verse 19. Number the ten plagues in this way. When there is a succession of promises or charges in a verse, it is better to write the numbers small at the beginning of each separate promise. Thus, there is a sevenfold promise to Abraham in Genesis 12:2–3: "(1) I will make you a great nation; (2) I will bless you; (3) and make your name great; (4) and you shall be a blessing;

(5) I will bless those who bless you; (6) and I will curse him who curses you; (7) and in you all the families of the earth shall be blessed." In Proverbs 1:22, we have (1) "simple ones," (2) "scorners," and (3) "fools."

Put an *X* in the margin against things not generally observed: for example, the laws regarding women wearing men's clothes, and regarding bird-nesting, in Deuteronomy 22:5–6; the sleep of the poor man and of the rich man compared in Ecclesiastes 5:12.

I also find it helpful to mark the following:

⬧ Cross-references. *For instance, opposite Genesis 1:1, write "By faith, Hebrews 11:3," because there we read: "By faith we understand that the worlds were framed by the word of God." Opposite Genesis 28:12, write "An answer to prayer, Genesis 35:3." Opposite Matthew 6:33, write "1 Kings 3:13" and "Luke 10:42," which give illustrations of seeking the kingdom of God first. Opposite Genesis 37:7, write "Genesis 50:18," which is the fulfillment of the dream.*

⬧ Railroad connections, that is, connections made by fine lines running across the page. *In Daniel 6, connect "will deliver" (verse 16), "able to deliver" (verse 20), and "has delivered" (verse 27). In Psalm 66, connect "come and see" (verse 5) with "come and hear" (verse 16).*

⬧ Variations of different translations. *For example, Romans 8:26 reads "the Spirit Himself" in the American Standard Version, not "itself" in the King James Version.*

- ❖ Unfortunate divisions of chapters. *The last verse of John 7 reads—"And everyone went to his own house." Chapter 8 begins "But Jesus went the mount of Olives." There ought to be no division of chapters here.*

- ❖ A short summary of the book's contents. *At the beginning of every book write something like the summary given in some Bibles at the head of every chapter.*

- ❖ Key words and key verses.

- ❖ A note of any text that marks a religious crisis in your life. *I heard Rev. F. B. Meyer preach on 1 Corinthians 1:9, and he asked his hearers to write on their Bibles that they were that day "called into the fellowship of His Son, Jesus Christ our Lord."*

TAKING SERMON NOTES

When a preacher gives out a Bible text, mark it; as he goes on preaching, put a few words in the margin, key words that shall bring back the whole sermon again. By that plan of making a few marginal notes, I can remember sermons I heard years ago. Every man ought to take down some of the preacher's words and ideas, and go into some lane or byway, and preach them again to others. We ought to have four ears— two for ourselves and two for other people. Then, if you are in a new town, and have nothing else to say, jump up and say: "I heard someone say this." Men will always be glad to hear you if you give them heavenly food. The world is perishing for lack of it.

Some years ago I heard a Briton in Chicago preach from a curious text, Proverbs 30:24–28, which begins with the verse:

"THERE ARE FOUR THINGS WHICH ARE LITTLE ON THE EARTH, BUT THEY ARE EXCEEDINGLY WISE."

Well, I said to myself, *what will you make of these "little things"? I have seen them a good many times.*

Then he went on speaking: "The ants are a people not strong, yet they prepare their food in the summer." He said God's people are like the ants. *Well,* I thought, *I have seen a good many of them, but I never saw one like me.*

"They are like the ants," he said, "because they are laying up treasure in heaven, and preparing for the future; but the world rushes madly on, and forgets all about God's command to lay up for ourselves incorruptible treasures.

"The rock badgers are a feeble folk, yet they make their homes in the crags," he continued; and then he explained: "Small rock badgers are very weak things; if you were to throw a stick at one of them you could kill it; but they are very wise, for they build their houses in rocks, where they are out of harm's way. And God's people are very wise, although very feeble; for they build on the Rock of Ages, and that Rock is Christ."

Well, I said, *I am certainly like the badgers.*

Then came the next verse: "The locusts have no king, yet they all advance in ranks [bands in KJV]." I wondered what he was going to make of that. "Now God's people," he said, "have no king down here. The world said, 'Caesar is our king'; but he is not our king. Our king is the Lord of Hosts. The locusts went out by bands; so do God's people. Here is a Presbyterian band, here an Episcopalian band, here a Methodist band, and so on; but by and by the great King will come and catch up all these separate ranks, and they will all be one, one fold and one Shepherd."

And when I heard that explanation, I said, *I would be like the locusts.* I have become so sick, my friends, of this miserable sectarianism, that I wish it could all be swept away.

"Well," he went on again, "the spider skillfully grasps with its hands, and it is in kings' palaces." When he got to the spider, I said, *I don't like that at all; I don't like the idea of being compared to a spider.*

"But," he said, "if you go into a king's palace, there is the spider hanging on his gossamer web, and looking down with scorn and contempt on the gilded salon; he is laying hold of things above. And so every child of God ought to be like the spider, and lay hold of the unseen things of God. You see, then, my brethren, we who are God's people are like the ants, the little badgers, the locusts, and the spiders—little things, but exceedingly wise."

I put that in the margin of my Bible, and the recollection of it does me as much good now as when I first heard it.

TAKING NOTES ON KEY VERSES AND CHAPTERS

In your own Bible study of key verses and chapters, take notes on what the Scripture says. For example, look at Isaiah 41:10: "Fear not, for I am with you; be not dismayed, for I am your God. I will strengthen you, yes, I will help you, I will uphold you with my righteous right hand." Mark what God says:

- ❖ *He is* with *His servant.*
- ❖ *He is* Isaiah's God.
- ❖ *He will* strengthen.
- ❖ *He will* help.
- ❖ *He will* uphold.

As another example, look at Psalm 103:2: "Bless the Lord, O my soul, and forget not all His benefits." If you cannot remember them all, remember what you can. In the next three verses there are five things:

- ❖ *Who* forgives *all your iniquities.*
- ❖ *Who* heals *all your diseases.*
- ❖ *Who* redeems *your life from destruction.*

❖ *Who* crowns *you with lovingkindness and tender mercies.*

❖ *Who* satisfies *your mouth with good things.*

From this same psalm we can learn some things about the mercy of the Lord :

❖ *Its quality: "tender" (verse 4).*

❖ *Its measure: "abounding" (verse 8).*

❖ *Its magnitude: "great," "as the heavens are high above the earth" (verse 11).*

❖ *Its duration: "from everlasting to everlasting" (verse 17).*

Turn to Isaiah 32, and mark four things that God promises in verse 2: "A man will be as a hiding place from the wind, and a cover from the tempest, as rivers of water in a dry place, as the shadow of a great rock in a weary land." There we have:

❖ *the hiding place from danger.*

❖ *the cover from the tempest.*

❖ *rivers of water.*

❖ *the Rock of Ages.*

In verses 3–4 of the same chapter you will read: "The eyes of those who see will not be dim, and the ears of those who hear will listen. Also the heart of the rash will understand knowledge, and the tongue of the stammerers will be ready to speak plainly." As you look for key words in your study, you will find that we have *eyes, ears, heart,* and *tongue* all ready to pay homage to the King of Righteousness.

NOTE TAKING ON PSALM 23

I suppose I have heard as many good sermons on Psalm 23 as on any other six verses in the Bible. I wish I had begun to take notes on them years ago when I heard the first one. Things slip away from you when you get to be fifty years of age. Young men had better go into training at once.

You can mine many jewels in your personal study and taking of notes on Psalm 23. Here is just one, based on the six verses of this compact but full psalm:

- ❖ *With me, the Lord.*
- ❖ *Beneath me, green pastures.*
- ❖ *Beside me, still waters.*
- ❖ *Before me, a table.*
- ❖ *Around me, mine enemies.*
- ❖ *After me, goodness and mercy.*
- ❖ *Ahead of me, the house of the Lord.*

"Blessed is the day," says an old divine, "when Psalm twenty-three was born!" It has been more used than almost any other passage in the Bible. Indeed, here is another way you may divide this rich psalm:

- ❖ *A happy life (verse 1).*
- ❖ *A happy death.*
- ❖ *A happy eternity.*

153

TAKING NOTES ON NEW TESTAMENT PASSAGES

Now turn into the New Testament and consider note taking in the Gospels. In John 4:47–53, the story of the nobleman suggests how a spiritual seeker can find the answer.

❖ *The nobleman* heard *about Jesus.*

❖ *He* went *unto Him.*

❖ *He* besought *Him.*

❖ *He* believed *Him.*

❖ *He* knew *that his prayer was answered.*

Again, in Matthew 11:28–30, we can learn about how to find the answer. The passage reads: "Come to Me, all you who labor and are heavy laden, and I will give you rest. Take My yoke upon you and learn from Me, for I am gentle and lowly in heart, and you will find rest for your souls. For My yoke is easy and My burden is light."

Someone has said these verses contain the only description we have of Christ's heart.

❖ *Something to do: come to Jesus.*

❖ *Something to leave: your burden.*

❖ *Something to take: His yoke.*

❖ *Something to find: rest for your soul.*

LENDING YOUR BIBLE

Don't be afraid to lend your Bible. Some people are; they worry the other person will mark up their Bibles. Well, welcome such marks; you can learn from them. Some time ago a man wanted to take my Bible home to get a few things out of it, and when it came back I found this noted in it:

Justification, *a change of state, a new standing before God.*
Repentance, *a change of mind, a new mind about God.*
Regeneration, *a change of nature, a new heart from God.*
Conversion, *a change of life, a new life for God.*
Adoption, *a change of family, new relationship toward God.*
Sanctification, *a change of service, separation unto God.*
Glorification, *a new state, a new condition with God.*

In the same handwriting I found these lines:

Jesus only; the light of heaven is the face of Jesus.
The joy of heaven is the presence of Jesus.
The melody of heaven is the name of Jesus.
The theme of heaven is the work of Jesus.
The employment of heaven is the service of Jesus.
The fullness of heaven is Jesus Himself.
The duration of heaven is the eternity of Jesus.

SUGGESTIONS ON MARKING A BIBLE

Here are some dos and don'ts as you begin to mark passages in a Bible:

- ❖ *Do not buy a Bible that you are unwilling to mark and use. An interleaved Bible gives room for notes.*
- ❖ *Be precise and concise. For example, Nehemiah 13:18 could be marked, "A warning from history."*
- ❖ *Never mark anything because you saw it in someone else's Bible. If it does not come home to you, if you do not understand it, do not put it down.*
- ❖ *Never pass a nugget by without trying to grasp it. Then mark it down.*

CHAPTER FIFTEEN

PERSONAL WORK FOR THE KINGDOM

DEALING PERSONALLY WITH THE LOST is of the most vital importance. No one can tell how many persons have been lost to the kingdom of God through lack of following up the preaching of the Gospel by personal work. Few church members are qualified to deal with inquirers, yet that is the very work in which they ought most efficiently to aid the pastor. People are not usually converted under the preaching of the minister. It is in the inquiry meeting that they are most likely to be brought to Christ. They are perhaps awakened under the minister, but God generally uses some other person to point out the way of salvation and bring the anxious to a decision.

We read about inquirers all through the Bible. When John the Baptist was preaching, he was interrupted. The only way to make sure that people understand what the minister is talking about is to let them ask questions. The Philippians jailor asked Paul and Silas, "What must I do to be saved?" Such questions can do more good than anything else. They can awaken a spirit of inquiry. Some of Christ's blessed teachings were called forth by questions.

This requires Christian workers who know the Scriptures and how to answer questions. We have thousands and thousands of church members who are good for nothing toward extending the kingdom of God. They understand bazaars, and fairs, and sewing-circles; but when you ask them to sit down and show a man or woman the way into God's kingdom, they say, "Oh, I am not able to do that. Let the deacons do it, or someone else."

BY YOUR KNOWLEDGE OF THE BIBLE,
YOU CAN BE PASSING ON
THE GOOD NEWS.

That is all wrong. The church ought to be educated on this very point. There are a great many church members who are just hobbling about on crutches. They can just make out that they are saved, and imagine that is all that constitutes a Christian. As far as helping others is concerned, that never enters their heads. They think if they can get along themselves, they are doing amazingly well. They have no idea what the Holy Spirit wants to do through them.

No matter how weak you are, God can use you; and you cannot say what a stream of salvation you may set in motion. John the Baptist was a young man when he died; but he led Andrew to Christ, and Andrew led Peter, and so the river flowed on.

By your knowledge of the Bible, you can be passing on the good news to others. This is a great way to profit from your study of the Bible.

SPREADING THE GOSPEL FOUND IN SCRIPTURES

Every believer, whether minister or layman, is duty-bound to spread the Gospel. "Go into all the world and preach the gospel to every creature" (Mark 16:15) was the wide command of our parting Savior to His disciples. There are many Bible students, however, who utterly neglect the command. They are like sponges always sucking in the Water of Life, but never imparting it to thirsty souls around.

A clergyman used to go hunting, and when his bishop reproved him, he said he never went hunting when he was on duty.

"When is a clergyman off duty?" asked the bishop.

And so with every Christian: When is he off duty?

To be ready with a promise for the dying, a word of hope for the bereaved and afflicted, of encouragement for the downhearted, of advice for the anxious, is a great accomplishment. The opportunities to be useful in these ways are numerous. Not only in inquiry meetings and church work, but in our everyday contact with others the opening constantly occurs. A word, a look, a handclasp, a prayer, may have unending influence for good. Knowing and using the Scriptures in these settings always helps too.

I admit one can't lay down positive rules in dealing with individuals about their religious condition. Tin soldiers are exactly alike, but not so men. Matthew and Paul were a good way apart. The people we deal with may be widely different. What would be medicine for one might be poison for another. In Luke 15:11–32, the elder son and the younger son were exactly opposite. What would have been good counsel for one might have been ruin for the other.

God never made two persons to look alike. If we had made humans, we probably would have made them all alike, even if we had to crush some bones to get them into the mold. But that is not God's way. In the universe there is infinite variety. The Philippian jailer required peculiar treatment. Christ dealt with Nicodemus one way, and the woman at the well another way.

With that in mind, here are a few guidelines in dealing with inquirers.

USING PERSONAL EXPERIENCE

It is a great mistake, in dealing with inquirers, to tell your own experience. Experience may have its place, but I don't think it has its place when we are dealing with inquirers; for the first thing the man you are talking to will do will be to look for your experience. He doesn't want your experience. He wants one of his own.

Suppose Bartimeus had gone to Jerusalem to the man who was born blind, and said, "Now, just tell us how the Lord cured you."

The Jerusalem man might have said, "He just spat on the ground and anointed my eyes with the clay."

"Ho!" says Bartimeus, "I don't believe you ever got your sight at all. Who ever heard of such a way as that? Why, to fill a man's eyes with clay is enough to put them out!"

Both men were blind, but they were not cured alike. A great many men are kept out of the kingdom of God because they are looking for somebody else's experience—the experience their grandmother had, their aunt, or someone in the family.

MEETING WITH ONE INQUIRER

Second, it is very important to deal with one inquirer at a time. A doctor doesn't give cod-liver oil for all complaints. "No," he says, "I must seek what each one needs." He looks at the tongue, and inquires into the symptoms. One may have the flu, another typhoid fever, and another tuberculosis. What a man needs is to be able to read his Bible, and to read human nature, too.

Those do best who do not run from one person in an inquiry meeting to another, offering words of encouragement everywhere. They would do better by going to but one or two an afternoon or evening. We are building for eternity and can take time. The work will not be superficial then.

Try first to win the person's confidence, and then your words will have more weight. Use great tact in approaching the subject.

It will be a great help to divide persons into classes as much as possible, and bring certain passages of Scripture to bear upon these classes. It is unwise, however, to use verses that you have seen in books until you are perfectly clear in your own mind of their meaning and application. Avail yourself by all means of suggestions from outside sources, but as David could not fight in Saul's armor, so you possibly may not be able to make good use of texts and passages that have proved powerful in the hands of another.

The best way is to make your own classification and select suitable texts, which experience will lead you to adopt or change, according to circumstances. Make yourself familiar with a few passages, rather than have a hazy and incomplete idea of a large number.

The following classification may be found helpful:

- Believers who lack assurance; who are in darkness because they have sinned; who neglect prayer, Bible study, and other means of grace; who are in darkness because of an unforgiving spirit; who are timid or ashamed to confess Christ openly; who are not engaged in active work for the Master; who lack strength to resist temptation and to stand fast in time of trial; who are not growing in grace.
- Believers who have backslidden.
- Those who are deeply convicted of sin and are seeking salvation.
- Those who have difficulties of various kinds. Many believe that they are so sinful that God will not accept them, that they have sinned away their opportunities and now it is too late, that the Gospel was never intended for them. Others are kept back by honest doubts regarding the divinity of Christ or the genuineness of the Bible. Others again are troubled by the mysteries of the Bible, the doctrines of election, instant conversion, etc., or they say they have sought Christ in vain, that they have tried and failed; they are afraid they could not hold out. A large class is in great trouble about feelings.
- Those who make excuses. There is a wide difference between a person who has a reason and one who had an excuse to offer. The commonest excuses are that there are so many inconsistent Christians, hypocrites in the church; that it would cost too much to become Christians, that they could not continue in their present occupation, etc.;

that their companions hold them back, or would cast them off if they were converted.

- ❖ *Those who are not convicted of sin. Some are deliberately sinful; they want to "see life," to "sow their wild oats." Others are thoughtless; others again are simply ignorant of Jesus Christ and His work. A large number do not feel their need of a Savior because they are self-righteous, trusting to their own morality and good works.*
- ❖ *Those who hold different creeds, embracing sectarians, cranks, spiritualists, infidels, atheists, agnostics, and so forth.*

USING YOUR BIBLE AND PRAYER

Third, always use your Bible in personal dealing. Do not trust to memory, but make the person read the verse for himself. Do not use printed slips or books. Hence, if convenient, always carry a Bible or New Testament with you.

Fourth, it is a good thing to get a man on his knees (if convenient), but don't get him there before he is ready. You may have to talk with him two hours before you can get him that far. But when you think he is about ready, say, "Shall we not ask God to give us light on this point?" Sometimes a few minutes in prayer have done more for a man than two hours in talk. When the Spirit of God has led him so far that he is willing to have you pray with him, he is not very far from the kingdom.

Ask him to pray for himself. If he doesn't want to pray, let him use a Bible prayer; get him to repeat it; for example, "Lord, help me!" Tell the man: "If the Lord helped that poor woman, He will help you if you make the same prayer. He will give you a new heart if you pray from the heart."

Don't send a man home to pray. Of course he should pray at home, but I would rather get his lips open at once. It is a good thing for a man to hear his own voice in prayer. It is a good thing for him to pray: "God, be merciful to me a sinner!"

DO THE WORK BOLDLY

Urge an immediate decision, but never tell a man he is converted. Never tell him he is saved. Let the Holy Spirit reveal that to him. You can shoot a man and see that he is dead, but you cannot see when a man receives eternal life. You can't afford to deceive one about this great question. But you can help his faith and trust, and lead him aright.

Always be prepared to do personal work. When war was declared between France and Germany, Count von Moltke, the German general, was prepared for it. Word was brought to him late at night, after he had gone to bed. "Very well," he said to the messenger, "the third portfolio on the left"; and he went to sleep again.

Do the work boldly. Don't take those in a position in life above your own, but as a rule, take those on the same footing. Don't deal with a person of opposite sex, if it can be otherwise arranged. Bend all your endeavors to answer for poor, struggling souls that question of all importance to them, "What must I do to be saved?"